CRITICAL ISSUES IN

STUDENT PERSONNEL WORK

CRITICAL ISSUES IN
STUDENT PERSONNEL WORK

A Problems Casebook

LAWRENCE LITWACK
Kent State University

JUNE E. HOLMES
Boston University

JANE S. O'HERN
Boston University

RAND MCNALLY & COMPANY . CHICAGO

Rand McNally Education Series
B. Othanel Smith, Advisory Editor

When you are so devoted to doing what is right that you press straight on to that and disregard what men are saying about you, there is the triumph of moral courage.

Phillips Brooks

PREFACE

This book is written for the purpose of bridging the gap between theory and practice in student personnel services. Too often, due to the stress on theoretical aspects, the desirable effects of actual practice (with the concomitant inward look) are postponed or eliminated from programs. Thus, the authors hope that this book will lead both the instructor and the student towards a more functional approach to guidance services.

Any approach to the problem of preparing the personnel worker must clearly distinguish between the techniques that have been found useful in similar situations, and the basic attitudes of the person who utilizes these, or any, techniques. The principles and practices which are offered to the student may expose him to new ways of viewing others. However, new ideas too often remain externalized, rather than being internalized and becoming an integral part of one's professional role. Growth involves a fundamental shift in position, and actually amounts to a change in personality structure or value system. Within any individual such change is frequently met with resistance, either latent or overt. For this reason, the cases in this book are designed to stimulate an analysis of one's attitudes and practices, and, hopefully, to encourage self-awareness and a new freedom of thought and action on the part of the personnel worker.

L. L.
J. E. H.
J. S. O'H.

TABLE OF CONTENTS

INTRODUCTION

The meaning and role of student personnel services in schools, colleges, and similar institutions involved with groups and individuals can be examined from a number of points of view. An awareness of these differences as they are viewed by leaders in the profession has recently been manifest in position papers at national conventions and in articles in the *Personnel and Guidance Journal*. At the same time, there has been a definite increase in criticism by the public at large. On the national level, there is opposition to and questioning of both theory and practice by such people as John Hersey in *The Child Buyers*, Martin Gross in *The Brain Watchers*, Banesh Hoffman in *The Tyranny of Testing*, Martin Mayer in *The Schools*, and James Koerner in *The Miseducation of American Teachers*,[1] to say nothing of the material contained in statements by Admiral Hyman Rickover and James B. Conant.

On the local level, individuals make statements denouncing personnel workers as "parasites feeding on a school system." As a result, personnel workers have been forced into a detailed self-examination, not only of their services but of their profession. Although any program will, of necessity, be heavily influenced by the philosophy of those responsible for the local planning and administration of such services, the place of the services themselves in the total developmental process is becoming more clearly defined.[2] The

---

[1] John Hersey, *The Child Buyers* (New York: Knopf, 1960); Martin Gross, *The Brain Watchers* (New York: Random House, 1962); Banesh Hoffman, *The Tyranny of Testing* (New York: Crowell-Collier, 1962); Martin Mayer, *The Schools* (New York: Harper, 1961); James D. Koerner, *The Miseducation of American Teachers* (Boston: Houghton Mifflin, 1963).
[2] C. Gilbert Wrenn, *The Counselor in a Changing World* (Washington: American Personnel and Guidance Association, 1962).

emphasis placed upon such services will vary with the over-all needs of the group, but, essentially, the focus of all personnel services should be the whole person in the total situation, i.e., the social, emotional, spiritual, physical, and intellectual aspects of the developmental process. Personnel workers in all fields of specialization and at all levels of administrative responsibility must be concerned with the needs and differences of people, and also with the social significance of behavior in our increasingly complex society. The nature of the school environment as a medium for the proper development of healthy personalities is of tremendous importance, and the fulfillment of an educational program depends greatly upon the attitudes, methods, and philosophy of those in a supervisory capacity.

One vital objective of any personnel services program is that it should enable the individual to assume an ever-increasing degree of responsibility for himself. Good guidance at any level is an adjustive process, and must be an integral and functioning part of any system concerned with the needs of the individuals under its care. To be successful, the process must be continuously concerned with the development of people as total personalities, able to function within their present and future environments. To achieve this end, the personnel worker must develop skills in understanding behavior, must possess sensitivity to the individual's needs, and must allow freedom for personal growth.

The problem of how to reach this objective most effectively is the constant concern of those involved in the preparation of personnel workers. The authors are all too aware that well-stated philosophical ideas and ideals frequently miscarry at an operational level. How is it possible to successfully combine theory and practice early in the training of student personnel workers without treating both superficially? Answers to such questions are currently being pursued by the Association of Counselor Education and Supervision, a division of the American Personnel and Guidance Association.

The rationale underlying personnel work is too broad and too involved to be covered in this book. For this reason, the bibliography in the appendix is designed to fulfill several functions: first, to provide resource materials for those who desire a more thorough foundation in the various theories; second, to examine the treatment of the cases in light of "expert" opinions; third, to compare and contrast the numerous approaches to the same ultimate objective— the optimum development of the individual.

PROBLEM-SOLVING

It has been widely demonstrated that participation is one of the most effective methods of achieving communication and cooperation.[3] Any one of several group techniques such as buzz groups, role-playing, or panel discussions might be used to effect the exploration and sharing of a variety of opinions. In contrast to these group procedures, the autocratic method may seem more efficient (i.e., responsibility and authority are clearly defined, discipline problems are reduced to a minimum, and an immediate solution can be found). However, when we consider this latter method from the viewpoint of the learning experiences inherent in participation, new-found rights of the individual, and shared decision-making, we frequently find none of these goals actually accomplished. Instead, value judgments and previous experiences interfere with new approaches. Principles of democratic interaction receive only lip-service, even though new problems often arise as a result of autocratic actions. Sometimes, administrative necessity is the rationale for a decision (fines imposed, privileges removed, suspension, etc.), with little apparent realization that it can hardly be considered helpful to the developmental process.

The major criticisms of the democratic procedure revolve around the arguments that it takes too much time, presents too many ideas, and introduces too many variables as far as individual contributions are concerned. The paradox in this situation is that the autocratic method may ultimately involve more problem-solving than would the democratic approach. Although the former may seem easier and more expedient in finding an immediate solution, the results are rarely lasting or desirable in the test of time. If the social signifi-

---

[3] G. C. Browne and Thomas S. Cohn, *The Study of Leadership* (Danville, Ill.: Interstate Publishers, 1958).

cance of experience is to be worth while, the personnel worker must provide a climate conducive to freedom for growth. The person who has difficulty interacting with others, either because of his own limitations or because of imposed leadership, will not be free to participate responsibiy in his society. When this happens, personnel workers have failed in their obligation to and relationship with such a person.

It is not the authors' intention to discourage the use of any of the previously mentioned methods, but rather to help the reader gain increasing awareness of the ways in which he handles various situations and the implications of the methods he uses. In actual situations such as faculty-student and employer-employee committee operations, we frequently find the appearance of shared responsibility. But, when the facts are examined, it becomes apparent that student and employee participation is kept at a minimum, and that decisions are made by those in authority: i.e., responsibility for implementing decisions is given to those who have had no voice in the decision-making. As a consequence, communication, individual responsibility, and personal initiative break down, often to the bewilderment of the administrator or decision-maker.

Freedom for decision-making is permitted in each of the cases presented in this book. If the problem itself is the attainment of a goal rather than the understanding of the causes of the problem, either the autocratic or democratic point of view may be equally appropriate. However, when, in the final analysis, only new problems ensue, then perhaps the method used by the central person should be re-examined.

Thus, the reader can evaluate his conclusions in terms of his personal responsibility and involvement, his community and its pressures, and his own philosophy of personnel work. As he analyzes the rationale behind his own suggested actions, and compares them with others in a group situation, he can openly express his own attitudes and needs. Discussion can be free, insight into other ways of viewing problems can be gained, and, ultimately, a broader understanding of the nature of the problem itself can be achieved. The risks inherent in any decision-making process are great, but our goal is not merely to have the reader find solutions to problems but, rather, to provide experiences that will encourage growth. This is the only way to insure freedom for individual thinking and creative approaches. If providing a climate of free expression can help to reduce hostility and resistance, then the personnel worker will be fulfilling his true role as educator.

THE CASE STUDY METHOD

Through personal experience in their own classes, the authors have found that the case study method has been extremely effective as a structured stimulus allowing relatively unstructured responses. Presenting a case for class and group discussion without prior assignment enables the observer to note the immediate responses of group members and the dynamics of group interaction. The case acts as a stimulus encouraging students to react as they feel they would if actually faced with the same situation. Attitudes and needs become evident, and the subsequent evaluation may lead to greater insight and growth on the part of each participant.

Another method is the assignment of cases in advance, requiring each group member to prepare a written analysis of how he would handle the problem. This serves the threefold purpose of allowing the instructor to become better acquainted with each student's philosophy, to introduce dynamic group interactions, and to evaluate the growth of each group member.

The cases have also been used as a springboard for role-playing. Class members act as the case subjects, while other students act as the central figure reacting to the problems presented. The realistic value of this method readily becomes apparent as the role-players gain insight into the total dynamics of the problem. This is especially important when one realizes how often we speak idealistically about how one would or should react in a given situation, rather than allowing ourselves to become personally involved.

Interviewing has long been an accepted procedure for screening job applicants, and recently, this method has been a prerequisite for acceptance into many graduate programs. The typical result is stilted interviews due to the candidate's over-cautiousness and desire to present himself in the best possible manner. Because of the artificial situation, the objective of getting to know more about the person often remains unfulfilled. If a discussion case were introduced into such a setting, the interviewer would have a more accurate and realistic basis for evaluating an individual or a group. His total recommendation would then rest not just upon impersonal academic records or subjective appraisals of experience and personality characteristics, but also upon a recognition of values which might affect a candidate's adjustment to the situation.

Other uses for the case study approach have included promoting discussion of problem areas by PTA groups or offering opportunities for self-expression in group guidance classes.

In order to amplify the previous suggestions, consider the following instance: One case was selected and given to twenty undergraduate seniors enrolled in an introductory guidance course. Each student received a copy of the case and was asked to write reactions to it and suggestions for handling the situation. At the following class meeting, the members were assigned to subgroups of five to share their various reports. Each subgroup taped its discussion and later these were played for the entire class in a further exchange of ideas and opinions. One of the taped sessions is presented in part in the Appendix. This particular subgroup comprised four women and one man, all seniors. Three of the women were education majors; the other two group members were liberal arts majors minoring in education.

In this situation, the group was given freedom to focus on any aspect of the problem which seemed important to them. A review of the transcript suggests a variety of analyses. One might look first at the dynamics of the group as its members discussed their feelings about the case. In other words, if the instructor wished to look at this meeting from a group-process point of view, he might analyze group behavior, roles played, degree of cohesiveness, movement, interaction, and so on. For example, he might attempt to determine if members perceived the central problem as a group, or if there was a relationship between group effectiveness and group leadership, and if there was free communication among members.

A second possible use of the taped session might be to analyze the content of the discussion. Do some of the responses reveal basic attitudes and personal values of the participants? What level of sophistication do the responses reveal? Where was the greatest emphasis—on the roommates, the incident, the accused, the staff, or on the reputation of the school? Did the case provide more than an intellectual experience? With answers to these questions, the instructor will have additional and helpful knowledge as he attempts to evaluate each individual's professional competence and potential.

Another way in which this case could have been presented to the group would have been for the instructor to construct a series of questions developed to focus the group's thinking in a specific direction. By doing this, he could have been certain that the discussion would cover the major points that he felt needed to be stressed. Thus, he would have had some basis for evaluating students' responses and would have been able to lead a depth discussion of some of the concepts underlying the questions. He might have asked the group to consider the legal aspects of this situation with respect to the responsibility of: (a) The college when violation of regulations are suspected which may affect the welfare and safety of residents; (b) The college when students search the personal property of others; (c) The professional role of the counselor.

These illustrations are presented as suggestions of ways in which a case may be utilized, and by no means exhaust the further exploration of the types of analyses. Our group of senior students could just as easily have been persons being interviewed for admission or employment, a personnel seminar section, a residence hall staff's in-service training meeting, or any other group of people involved with interpersonal relations. The "ideal" use of the case study method will be dependent upon the objectives, philosophy, and creativity of the individual instructor.

SUMMARY

Once one leaves the theoretical aspects of personnel services, he is immediately confronted with the problem of reality; that is, adapting the theory he has been taught to the problems he is experiencing in the daily practice of his profession. Beginning students may find themselves adopting the philosophy of the school they are attending without really understanding either the rationale behind the philosophy or its practical application in everyday situations. Sometimes, the originality and creativity of the student is stifled if he is limited to certain preconceived ideas stressed by his instructor as being the "right" way to handle the problem. The authors have prepared this book in an attempt to stimulate imaginative approaches to problems, approaches completely unhampered by the traditional bonds of conservatism or custom.

After this brief introduction, the authors present the following cases, with the accompanying hope that they will prove as successful elsewhere in the future as they have for the authors in the past. The majority of these cases were drawn from real situations encountered by personnel workers in the field. Others were written specifically to spotlight critical aspects of student personnel work such as legality and confidentiality. The focus of each case is twofold: first, rather than dramatize, it seemed desirable to strip each situation to its essential points, ending with the need for a thoughtful evaluation by the reader; second, rather than limiting student thinking to specific points of concern, it is hoped that the lack of structure will mean freedom to examine the case's implications for personnel work in its entirety.

The reader will note that each case ends with one or more specific questions. If one focuses only upon an immediate solution, he may run the risk of overlooking many alternatives present in the situation. Too frequently, judgments or suggestions are made with little thought for the multiple variations inherent in the situation. The reader is encouraged to consider and to evaluate *all* possible approaches as he assumes the role of central person in each case. Some of the conflicts with which he may be confronted should help him attain a clearer delineation of the professional responsibilities of the personnel worker.

PART I

CRITICAL ISSUES: THE COMMUNITY

Society everywhere is in conspiracy against the Manhood of everyone of its members. Society is a joint-stock company in which the members agree, for the better securing of his bread to each shareholder, to surrender the liberty and culture of the eater. The virtue in most requests is conformity. Self-reliance is its aversion. It loves not realities and creators, but names and customs.

Ralph Waldo Emerson,
Self-Reliance

A democratic society recognizes that each member has certain "natural" or, at any rate, "constitutional" rights that will be restricted only when he violates the rights of others.

Robert B. Brode,
Issues in University Education

Educational institutions throughout the country have recently been faced with increasing community pressures. Community pressures dealing with problems of physical facilities, curriculum, integration, and other central issues have played a major role in creating new dimensions in educational planning. Although the public school is a state-mandated institution and the nature is specified by legislative action, many religious and civic groups have been instrumental in forging new school policies—sometimes in the crucible of criticism.

The function of educational leadership is to administer programs in the light of the expressed needs, abilities, and interests of the students in attendance. If education is to fulfill its purpose, it must point the way toward a better society by examining the problems in today's society. If its purpose is merely to reflect and perpetuate the *status quo,* then education is negligent and will be found wanting when tested by the perspective of time. Symptomatic of the new directions being investigated are newly developed units on Communism, narcotics, sex, alcoholism, and similar topics. Such efforts have received both favorable and unfavorable recognition. In some areas, it has not been unusual for school leaders to eliminate certain programs for fear of community criticism. It would seem that academic freedom is in jeopardy when community pressures are permitted to dictate, alter, or otherwise inhibit educational advancements or opportunities.

Parent-teacher associations have been a source of both support and criticism for schools moving in new directions. However, these groups do not completely solve the problem of person-to-person communication. The parent-teacher-counselor conference represents one attempt to improve communication in this area. During such a conference the professional worker is expected to provide information, present solutions, judge special requests, and interpret behavior. An examination of the content of these conferences would show the conflicts which most commonly arise are in the area of unrealistic goals—whether perceived from the parents' or the personnel worker's frame of reference. The greater the gap between the real self and the ideal self, the more likely is a breakdown in communiaction. If we agree that most parents view their child as an extension of themselves, we can readily understand their defensiveness and resistance to being made aware of their child's potentialities and limitations. In reviewing the content of many such conferences, it becomes apparent that all that may have been accomplished is an increase in the anxiety of both parent and child.

Conflict may also arise for the personnel worker when he tries to reconcile his responsibility to the student, his function within the school, and his role as perceived by the parent. The purpose of working with parents should be more than merely public relations or an attempt to gain a picture of home conditions, it should be a two-way communication—a sharing of how the child is seen by all concerned. Parental contacts can provide an excellent opportunity to facilitate mutual understanding of the child, as well as enabling the parent to gain insight into his role as it affects the child. Increased awareness of his own needs and interests and a greater perception of their relationship to his decisions and attitudes concerning the child are possible, and may result in the parent's giving the kind of assistance most helpful to the child.

Ethically, it is generally agreed that the counselor's first responsibility is to the client or counselee. Translating this into another set of circumstances, it is easy to foresee situations in which the professional worker may be unable to function without a full awareness of the legal implications of his actions. Obligations to society, to one's profession, and to the individual counselee may combine to place the counselor on the horns of a dilemma. The guidelines present to help him reach a decision are somewhat ambiguous, with the result that each counselor must reach his own decision. The American Psychological Association and the American Personnel and Guidance Association have similar codes of ethics relating to confidentiality. However, these statements do little more than point towards possible decision-making processes; final responsibility rests squarely on the counselor. This would seem to necessitate a careful program clarifying the ethical and legal aspects of counseling. Unfortunately, the majority of existing programs do little with this area except for an occasional seminar.

The role of the counselor places him in a position to receive not only information which relates to a client's past, present, or future behavior, but also information concerning the behavior of individuals known to the client. Other professions such as law, medicine, and the clergy have established the concept of *privileged communication*. Although laws differ from state to state, the protection offered by this concept allows all communication between the professional person and his client to remain confidential unless released by one of the parties to the communication.

The question of *legal immunity* has received but superficial attention from the service professions of counseling, psychology, and social work. Most states have yet to grant any semblance of immunity by virtue of privileged communication status to counseling activities. As a result, counselors are forced to make a moral choice—should they break a confidence to protect themselves from possible legal action if the counselee has revealed a violation of a law, or should they maintain a confidence at the risk of court action that might jeopardize their professional future? If legal immunity were provided for counselors, both they and the individuals with whom they work could feel secure in the knowledge that there were no restrictions on the security of material being discussed in counseling sessions.

One of the goals of the counseling process is to provide a relationship in which the client is enabled to realize and accept direction for his own behavior. In such a relationship, it may be desirable for the client to completely expose his behavior for discussion. If the professional worker is concerned with the extent to which he is assisting another to mock law and authority—if he is primarily concerned with his own liability in terms of communicated material—then his actions and responses to the counselee will be based more upon protecting himself from legal action, and he will actively and overtly interpret the implications of such behavior.

Not all behavior, however, is necessarily negative in terms of the law. There are times when the situation is one in which the counselor or the school may decide to take the responsibility for certain actions pertaining to the health and welfare of students.

The condition of *in loco parentis* has been widely used to justify institutional actions in a particular case. However, the question remains unanswered as to how much responsibility an institution should take, and the point at which the school's responsibility stops and the parent's takes over. The parent's willingness to assume responsibility might be greater if the institution were less willing to accept it. A prime example of this can be seen in the widespread practice of curfews for women students in colleges.

The last four cases in this section were selected to exemplify problem situations that lie within the area of the institution's responsibility *in loco parentis*. The issue at hand may be that of maintaining confidentiality, versus the decision not to aid and abet behavior contrary to the laws of society. Can the personnel worker both remain neutral or noncommittal with a counselee who has failed to accept social norms and, at the same time, demonstrate convictions that society has the right to expect certain behavior from its membership? Perhaps the ultimate definition of privileged communication lies in the personnel worker's willingness to be professional, and thus cannot be instituted by law.

In the cases within this section, there is seldom a single over-riding issue. Problems are complex, and as such require complex analyses. Frequently, "solution" may be the wrong goal; there may be none which is altogether satisfying. Individuals and their problems are much like images in a kaleidoscope—they present constantly changing and totally different pictures. By applying new approaches to old situations, perhaps we can find greater light and direction.

COMMUNITY PRESSURES, I

Cases 1–3 present problems dealing with the area of community pressure for or against existing problems, and the responsibility of the school in such cases. Case 1 revolves around the school's right to take a stand, and the obligation to respect the right of the individual. Case 2 deals with the result of poor public relations, the school's failure to provide for individual differences, and the counselor's role as mediator. Case 3 is concerned with a major issue in education today, that of a program forced upon a school and community against the wishes of the majority. It also raises the question of the right and ability of society to legislate morality.

CASE 1

You are a counselor in a suburban high school. At the annual June graduation, it is the tradition to announce the winners of various scholarship awards among the graduating seniors. One of these awards, a $1000 scholarship, is given annually by the Daughters of the American Revolution to the girl graduate with the highest scholastic average in United States history.

This year the student with the top average is the daughter of a family that recently arrived in this country as refugees. When the scholarship committee of the D.A.R. receives the name, it also manages to obtain the information that the girl is not a citizen of the United States. As a result, it refuses to award the scholarship to the girl, and asks for the name of the second ranking student. The issue finds its way into the local paper, and is promptly given national publicity by the various news services. The D.A.R. refuses to back down. What is your role in working with all concerned? From a personnel point of view, do you feel the school's responsibility is to protect the rights of the individual when it may mean taking a stand contrary to that expressed by a community group? If requested to do so, what position would you take for or against any school position in this situation?

CASE 2

As high school director of pupil personnel services, you have been called to a conference with the principal and the two women's physical education instructors. The topic under discussion is the type of showers which have been installed during the summer months. Due to the increased enrollment, a new gymnasium has been completed. In an effort to keep costs down, communal showers have been installed instead of the former shower stalls.

Shortly after the start of school, several girls refused to take showers under the new arrangement. The physical education instructors insist that all students take showers at the end of their class. They told the girls concerned that failure to do so would mean automatic failure of the course. When the students appealed to the principal, they were told that their objections were unreasonable.

The situation has now grown to community-wide proportions. A number of parents are expressing violent protests, and claim that the new showers provide no privacy, contribute to indecent behavior, and are too embarrassing to many of the girls. They have demanded that the Board of Education remove the physical education requirement for graduation, and that the course be made optional. The board has asked the principal for a complete report on the situation before acting on the parents' request.

As the chief personnel worker in the school, you are asked for your opinion. What would you suggest to try to resolve the dilemma? What might be done to prevent a similar situation from arising in the future? What would be your responsibility—if any—in working with concerned individuals?

CASE 3

You are the director of pupil personnel services for a metropolitan high school in one of the leading cities in the South. As a result of the Supreme Court decision, the Board of Education has ordered that ten Negro students be admitted to the twelfth grade of your previously all-white school. Although privately the members of the board share the prevailing community attitudes against integration, they had exhausted all legal possibilities and ordered the gradual desegregation of the public schools beginning with the twelfth grade and adding a grade a year. The local parochial schools have been totally desegregated for a year. Prior to the passage of the civil rights bill, the rest of the community was completely segregated.

Today, the opening day of school, you have been witnessing a battle against integration. Encouraged by adults, three-quarters of the student body have not attended classes, but have been demonstrating outside the school. The remaining white students in school have been engaging in subtle but effective harassment of the small group of new students. This has occurred with the knowledge and covert support of a small group of teachers.

As you review the events of the day, you are disheartened by what happened. This feeling is intensified by reports from teachers that many of the outstanding student leaders were in the front ranks of the strikers. In order to prevent a recurrence tomorrow, the Board of Education has contacted the local television station, requesting time to discuss the issues and problems. You have been asked to assist in the planning of the program. How do you view your role in such a situation? Does a personnel worker have a responsibility to participate in community issues? What effect might your actions have upon your relationships within the school?

COMMUNITY PRESSURES, II

At times, pressures from the community take the form of action by well-meaning but misdirected local groups. As a result, the school is forced to re-evaluate its public relations policy with a view towards restoring communication. This is particularly true when brought down to an individual basis. Groups such as parent-teacher associations have been of immeasurable help in communicating educational objectives and the desirability of parental cooperation with the school and individual personnel. Case 4 illustrates the type of problem that can ensue when communication is disrupted, and when there has been a failure in the clear delimitation of responsibility between the school and the cooperating group or agency.

CASE 4

You are the school psychologist for a growing suburban school system. Your community has an extremely active PTA group that has received national recognition for its contributions to education in the community. The group has been studying further ways to involve parents in the total educational program. The most recent proposal is for you to conduct a workshop for volunteers interested in helping youngsters with behavior and learning problems in the schools. The workshop would cover elementary testing principles as well as the psychodynamics of behavior. Cases in point would be drawn from the local system.

There is a great deal of opposition to this proposal, particularly from teachers and other guidance personnel who feel that the parents may do more harm than good, and that the group would be hindering their own professional work. You have been asked to prepare a statement of your views on this matter for the next PTA meeting. Would you consider your role to be objective or partisan? In light of your choice, what would you say? How would you try to resolve any resulting stalemate?

PARENTAL COMMUNICATION

Cases 5–7 represent typical problems faced by the personnel worker in interpreting realistically to parents the capacities of their children. Cases 5 and 6 present similar problems, in that part of the difficulty in both instances revolves around faulty public relations and ex post facto communication of a school decision. Case 7 deals more with the establishment of legitimate criteria for the identification of the exceptional child. The problem here is not one of defending such criteria, but rather of communicating them to all concerned.

CASE 5

You are a high school counselor in a predominantly professional community. It is an annual tradition in your school for the guidance department to sponsor a college night for juniors who are preparing for higher education and for seniors who have not yet made a specific choice. Parents are encouraged to attend with their sons and daughters, to meet with the various college representatives.

Three weeks in advance of the night, each student is given a list of the colleges which will be represented. Several colleges have asked that you limit the students attending their sessions to those who will be eligible for consideration. The major reason given is that more attention could then be given to those who were actually qualified. You have cooperated with this plan, and where necessary have approved only those students' choices which are more appropriate for them in light of their aptitude and previous achievement.

Two days before the actual night, the students receive their assignments accompanied by an invitation for their parents to attend. The next morning, an irate parent is waiting for you when you arrive at school, wanting to know why his son, a junior, wasn't given his collegiate choices. The boy in question had listed three highly competitive institutions even though his academic average was a straight C coupled with a completely undistinguished record.

It would appear that the student's choices were unrealistic, and so was the emotional reaction of the father. How might you proceed to assist both the father and son to arrive at a realistic level of academic planning and expectations? What might be done in the future to help prevent similar situations?

CASE 6

You are a guidance counselor in an elementary school. One of your responsibilities is participation on a five-man committee to select students for the gifted-child program. Prior to the selection, letters of explanation are sent to all parents clarifying the structure, objectives, and the general criteria of selection for the program. Parents who may not wish their children to be considered are encouraged to notify the principal. After the final choices have been made, an official letter is sent from the principal's office notifying all parents of their child's placement for the coming year.

Three days after the letters were sent, one of the parents storms into your office and demands to know more specifically the criteria for selection. According to a Stanford-Binet test score revealed to her by a student at a local university, her son had an IQ of 141 which placed him in the very superior range of intelligence. However, her son was not selected, and she demands to know why. Although she doesn't come right out and say so, she hints at political pressure and bias on the part of the selection committee. How would you handle this situation? What suggestions do you have to prevent such occurrences from arising in the future? What steps should be involved in the identification of the exceptional child?

CASE 7

For the past two years you have been the guidance counselor for an elementary school system. At the end of your first year, the administration and teachers gave unqualified sanction to your proposal to institute an intensive testing program starting in the first grade. Included in the over-all battery would be tests designed to measure reading readiness, reading comprehension, achievement, and intelligence.

As a general rule, written evaluations of each student prepared by your office are sent to the teachers and parents. However, for those students whose scores would seem to warrant special class placement, a conference with the parents is recommended.

You know from past experience that many parents find it difficult to accept the knowledge that their child is a slow learner or retarded. From the psychological aspect, you are aware that parents frequently view their children as an extension of themselves, and thus you anticipate their anxiety and hostility. This is complicated by the fact that you are a resident of the community, and thus know many of the parents socially.

The primary purpose of the interview is to promote a cooperative relationship between the school and the parents so that the individual child may be able to take advantage of the educational opportunities available to him. How would you prepare for an interview with the parents of a first grader whose scores and classroom performance seem to indicate his placement in the slow learning classroom?

THE TEACHER-COUNSELOR

Cooperation between the home and the school is essential if the individual is to profit from his educational experiences.

A few of the media presently employed for greater home-school communication are special orientation programs for parents, small group meetings, and child–parent–personnel worker conferences, in addition to the organized group programs. However, it is vital for the personnel worker to clearly define his role for himself as well as for the parent. When the personnel worker represents a dual role, confusion and conflict may easily result. Case 8 serves to illústrate the role conflict inherent in the teacher-counselor's position, particularly when others may see him in roles different from those which he perceives for himself.

CASE 8

You are a psychology instructor and part-time counselor at a coeducational college. At the end of the previous semester, fifteen students out of a class of 75 failed the advanced theories of personality course.

Early one afternoon, you return to your office after class and find one of the failed students waiting with her parents. The term ended seven weeks ago, and this is the first time you have seen the student since grades were issued. Her father states that they had been away on a six-weeks' business trip and had just been notified of the failure. He questions the basis for the grade. You explain that she failed to fulfill the course requirements which had been clearly defined in class as well as duplicated for each student at the start of the semester. He requests facts whereupon you indicate that her record on class work and examinations was below average, and that two-thirds of the written work had never been submitted.

Immediately the girl begins to cry, and interrupts by stating that she had left all the papers on your desk the afternoon prior to the final examination. You indicate that the work was not there and to date has not been received. However, you indicate a willingness to accept the carbons or original drafts. Again the girl bursts into tears and relates that these have been thrown away. The father calls you careless and states that this failure will cost his daughter her academic scholarship for the coming year. Although she will be entering her senior year, he cannot afford to aid her financially and the scholarship is essential. You are aware that any such grant will be out of the question since this course will affect her eligibility.

Often in such cases a person who functions with dual responsibilities, that is as both teacher and counselor, is forced to make a decision between the evaluative role or the therapeutic role. If you were in this position, which choice would you make? Discuss the rationale for your decision and the implications pertaining to it.

THE LAW AND THE COUNSELOR

Cases 9 and 10 raise the issue of *in loco parentis* and responsibility to the individual. Case 11 poses the problem of the school's legal responsibility for the welfare of the individual child under its supervision. Case 12 presents the pointed issue of responsibility to the individual versus responsibility to society. It serves to illustrate situations in which the counselor's personal judgment and philosophy are all-important in helping him deal with the situation.

CASE 9

You are the guidance counselor in a liberal arts college. A freshman student has failed to meet the academic standards of the school and therefore has been dismissed. During the exit interview held with all terminated students, the girl indicated to you that when she had called her parents to tell them of the school's action, they informed her that she is not to come home but is to remain at school. You report this to the dean who calls the parents to verify the student's statement, and to inform the parents officially of the school's action and the reason for it.

Again the parents refuse to accept this decision, and tell the dean that when the school accepted the girl, she became the school's responsibility and not the parents'. They refuse to take the girl out of school, and insist that it is the school's responsibility to help the girl stay in school. In reporting the conversation to you, the dean tells you that she has given the parents 24 hours to come to pick up their daughter. Otherwise, the girl is to be sent home by bus. She instructs you to notify the girl of the situation and get her ready to leave. How would you proceed to work with the girl? If the parents appear, how would you work with them? Does the school have any responsibility in such cases?

CASE 10

You are the counselor for a private residential secondary school. One Monday morning, when you arrive at your office, the headmaster is waiting to tell you that the local police have taken one of the school's senior students into custody for drunken driving and suspected hit-and-run. The youth has denied the charges, but facts gathered by the police seem to indicate his guilt. At a hearing, a thousand-dollar bail was set for the boy, and the headmaster is wondering whether or not the school should furnish bail funds.

The boy's parents are presently in Europe, and left word before they departed that the school should contact the boy's grandmother if anything came up before their return. Although they would be traveling widely, they would attempt to keep the grandmother informed of their whereabouts. They also plan to write regularly to their son, and have asked him to communicate regularly with his grandmother.

The parents have also asked that the grandmother not be contacted by the school except in case of absolute emergency because she is recovering from a coronary seizure. What is the school's legal responsibility, if any, in such a case? How would you proceed in the best interest of all concerned?

CASE 11

You are an elementary school counselor who has been requested to review the case of a sixth-grade boy. During the past year, he has been increasingly truant, and the most recent report by the attendance officer portrayed the boy's home conditions in a questionable light. In a conference with the school social worker and the attendance officer, it is decided to have the visiting teacher visit the home and make a complete report to you on home conditions.

Two days later, the visiting teacher presents her report, citing evidence of alcoholism, adultery, and gross negligence towards children in the home. She recommends that proceedings be immediately initiated to remove the boy from the home. What are the legal implications and procedures in such an action? How would you go about working with the parents if you felt this to be desirable? What should be the school's role in such a situation?

CASE 12

You are a guidance counselor in a metropolitan high school that has experienced increasing discipline problems with the students. Results of a survey completed by the school committee and read at a recent faculty meeting indicate that much of the difficulty seems to originate among students who have become addicted to narcotics. The chief of police, who was present at the meeting, urged the faculty to do everything possible to obtain names of individuals using and distributing narcotics. He promises faculty members legal immunity for any information obtained and given to him. The school committee wholeheartedly supports his plea.

The following week, during a counseling session, a 17-year-old senior asks your help in breaking the narcotics habit. He tells you that he obtained the drugs from a neighborhood store, but states that he could never reveal the source for fear of retaliation. He further states that he knows a number of classmates who are drug addicts. Keeping in mind your responsibilities to the individual, the community, and society, what would you do?

PART II

CRITICAL ISSUES: THE SCHOOL

The educator cannot evade the fundamental moral problems of our time, for education is concerned with values and ideal concepts. The work of the educator is incomplete as long as suffering, frustration, and want prevail. This is not a time for smugness or self-righteousness on the part of the educator.

Frederick Mayer,
*Philosophy of Education
for Our Time*

During the past decade great strides have been made in the field of education, but is this a guarantee that their direction has always been positive? It is true that the "little red school house" has been replaced by a more modern physical plant, and that rural districts are now consolidating in order to provide better learning environments for the students who do not happen to live in suburbia. But, perhaps it is time to stop and consider what is happening inside the multi-million-dollar structures. To be sure, more and more students are going to college—in fact, the statistics look quite impressive. It is currently stated that those who were fortunate enough to obtain an education ten or twenty years ago would probably have difficulty even being admitted to the same institutions today. The implication seems clear—the standards for today's students are sharply different than those of yesterday! This raises the question: What is the purpose of education? Is it mere memorization of facts, a high score on the College Entrance Examination Boards or the American College Test, or knowing the difference between "right" and "wrong"; or is it the freedom to be and the recognition of all the responsibilities that are coupled with this freedom? If one concurs with Barzun when he stated that "education comes from within; it is a man's own doing, or rather it happens to him—sometimes because of the teaching he has had, sometimes in spite of it . . .,"[1] then the criteria by which we are currently evaluating our schools seem completely out of focus. Often a school's annual report comments on the high percentage of the graduating class accepted for additional education, but seldom does a report focus on the growth of students as individuals.

The term "team approach" is probably one of the most misused in our era. What do we mean by a team—a group of people all working toward one goal, a number of groups competing with each other, or a group of individuals all going their own ways? Who are the team members—the parents, the administrators, the pupil personnel staff, the teachers? What about the students? The struggle to get on the "right" team seems appropriately expressed by Barzun:

---

[1] Jacques Barzun, *Teacher in America* (Boston: Little, Brown, 1945), p. 4.

Then begins the fierce, secret struggle out of which
education may come—the struggle between home and
school, parent and child, child and teacher; the struggle
also that lies within the parent and within the society
concerning the teacher's worth: Is this man of knowledge to be looked up to as wise and helpful, or to be
looked down on as at once servile and dangerous, capable and inglorious, higher than the parent yet lower
than the brat . . . .[2]

Why does a community have a school—to have a place to send the
child for twelve years, so that teachers will have a job, or because of
its need to conform with the neighboring community? Ideally,
everyone will agree that the school exists for the student and that
the job of the administrator, teacher, or member of the pupil personnel staff is only to aid in the enhancement of each individual.
Why then do educators allow personal needs to interfere with this
goal? It would seem that, if this goal were an article of belief and
not just another educational cliché, the conflicts faced by many
students could be alleviated.

John Donne once said, "No man is an island, entire of itself"[3]
and yet the administrator, the teacher and the personnel worker,
who may know and quote Donne, each seems to find refuge in his
own small area. Frequently, the personnel worker, because of the
nature of his work, fails to recognize that he must function with
the support of the administration under whom he is working and
the cooperation of the staff with whom he is associated. Recognition
of this situation may be the reason that most states require teaching
experience prior to certification of guidance and other personnel
workers, on the assumption that a person who has had classroom
experience may be more mindful of the need for communication
among all those responsible for educating students. Whether or not
this particular reasoning is valid is irrelevant, but the importance

[2] *Ibid.*, p. 5.
[3] John Donne, *Devotions*, XVII.

of communication among school personnel does warrant consideration.

The sharing of information among personnel workers, administrators, and faculty, without relinquishing confidentiality, may enable some situations to be handled more effectively. In-service training programs and assignments to *ad hoc* committees have been used to open channels of group communication. Even though these types of procedures sometimes seem to be more program-centered than student-centered, both are needed, and the professional worker is in an ideal position to contribute theoretical and experimental knowledge as well as democratic leadership. It is unfortunate that workers pay too little attention to their responsibility of participating in the over-all school environment, but seem more content to remain behind closed doors wishing for the evolution of different attitudes toward students.

The term "organization" is most commonly understood as meaning structure such as line-staff relationship, centralized or decentralized programs, or the generalist versus the specialist approach. Whatever the actual format, the primary focus is the same for all: the development of the individual's potential as a whole person. The individual seems to be best served when there is a cooperative atmosphere among all school personnel as well as a clear delineation of their respective responsibilities. But this ideal cooperative attitude is not always a reality; the major weakness of many organizational structures seems to be the ineffective procedures by which personnel share their understanding of students.

Too few guidance personnel are willing to discuss objectively some of the issues facing them in their work with youth, but resort to blaming the administration for their ineffectuality. Many educational practices continue despite contradictory findings provided by research in the field of the behavioral sciences. Reward and punishment are still considered important to motivation in learning; intelligence scores continue to be the main criterion for class grouping; and the socio-economic level remains a prime factor in college attendance. These are but a few; the reader can continue the list. Whether the personnel worker is pupil personnel administrator, guidance counselor, school psychologist, or psychometrist, it seems imperative that he act as a team member, sharing his knowledge with others, rather than standing on the side lines as a distant figure of authority. Even the best systems will fail when those with specific preparation deny their responsibility to help others understand the implications of conditions related to effective learning.

Contrary to the opinions of many, there is no *one* way to structure the guidance program. There is, however, more agreement as far as the types of services which should be offered: testing, group meetings, counseling, occupational exploration, etc. When these services should be offered and which ones should take precedence will be influenced by the educational philosophy, objectives of the curriculum, and the needs and interests of the students.

If we are concerned with the development of the whole person, we cannot fail to mention the nonacademic areas, such as student activities or housing, for they too are vital parts of the learning environment. A study of school curricula of the past shows that student activity programs are not a new phenomenon, but have long held a significant place in the educational milieu. This point is most clearly emphasized by the recent references to activities being "co-curricular" rather than "extra-curricular." Such opinions support the theory that student activities provide an arena in which the essentials of education and the process of human relations can be developed. Activities usually have administrative approval and faculty sponsorship, and are valued by most as an integral part of the overall educational setting.

The program and mandates of the co-curricular activities should meet the changes and influences of the times, and should be student-initiated, student-oriented, and student-centered. As long as activity programs fulfill the purposes for which they are designed, they are viewed as being worth while and student membership is encouraged. However, as some of the cases point out, such objectives are not always met. It is upon such occasions that the personnel worker is called in to give his professional assistance. His knowledge of human behavior and group dynamics can be beneficial in evaluating the proposals and their implications as they influence the lives of students. In this role of consultant, the personnel worker has the opportunity to promote an understanding of the responsibility each individual has to himself and the group—as well as to promote the acceptance of individuals by the group. Ideally, the activity program provides an experimental laboratory in which students are able to participate actively in a democratic situation.

Encouraging persons to work cooperatively toward a common purpose cannot be accomplished by a constitution or by-laws. Sensitivity to the needs and feelings of the self and to those of the group is a major aspect of group dynamics. It is difficult for some administrators and faculty members to realize that the result of a particular group project is actually secondary to the process by which decisions were reached. Student activities should provide for the creative development of the individual as well as create a laboratory in human relations and exemplify democracy in action.

Historically speaking, student quarters and living conditions have been minor concerns to most institutions of higher education. With the application of philosophies of education and the emphasis on the "whole man," housing has taken on a different significance and today represents a vital part of the student's educational experience.

The proper function of an educational institution as is the case with most service organizations, depends on the existence of a structure of authority and a clear delineation of how participants must behave. An examination of any residence hall handbook reveals not only the philosophical foundations and academic objectives of a particular institution, but also the institution's rules governing individual behavior. To be sure, limits are not explicitly defined; but they are implicitly noted. Depending upon the nature of an individual's behavior, the jurisdiction for hearing and determining sentence, if any, will be dictated by the organizational structure. Usually, less serious misdemeanors will be handled by the student government or its representative. However, because so many schools and colleges do assume responsibility of *in loco parentis,* the more difficult cases come under administrative review. Frequently, some type of action on the part of either committee is considered advisable so that others can see by example the degree of acceptance of individual behavior in a group situation. Administrators view the residence hall program as an extension of the classroom, personnel workers see it as a laboratory in human relations, and managerial staff consider it primarily a business venture. With these conflicting philosophies, it is little wonder that some of the residence programs reflect fragmented experiences.

A number of the cases in this section attempt to illustrate the complexity of the residence hall community and its effect upon individual adjustment. It would seem that more energy is spent attempting to define the residence hall program and the kind of resident who will benefit from such a program than is concerned with designing programs which will encourage individuals to search for self-identity within a group environment. The resident cannot be separated from himself and his world, nor can he be expected merely to conform to some format designed to help him exist while engaging in his academic and social pursuits. When this happens, the practice of education is being permitted to refute the theory.

ORGANIZATION AND ADMINISTRATION
OF PERSONNEL SERVICES

Cases 13–20 present situations in which the professional worker must examine means of facilitating a deeper understanding of his staff relationships with others, and in which he can question in depth some specific areas such as role clarification and program evaluation.

Cases 13 and 14 illustrate the need for internal and external role clarification by personnel workers. Better understanding of various personnel functions will allow both school personnel and the community to make greater use of personnel services. Cases 15 and 16 describe administrative problems in communicating with those in higher positions of authority, e.g., the superintendent of schools and the board of education or school committee. Case 17 deals with the need for continual re-evaluation of programs. Cases 18 and 19 are concerned with the internal administration of a pupil personnel program. Case 20 points up the role conflict for the personnel worker who is involved in administrative decision-making.

CASE 13

You have recently been appointed director of guidance in a high school serving 1200 students. Before your arrival, the guidance functions were handled by a dean of boys and a dean of girls. The principal has expressed to you the need for reorganizing the program with clear definition of responsibilities.

After several meetings with the two deans, it becomes very evident that all school personnel would benefit from a clearer explanation of what counselors do. The deans tell you of the petty discipline problems with which they have to cope. These and many similar situations tend to lower their position in the eyes of students and staff.

Realizing that faculty and administrative support and complete understanding of the functions of student personnel services are major factors in the success of any guidance program, how would you proceed in regard to all personnel concerned?

CASE 14

At a recent PTA meeting, several persons complained to you, as the school psychologist for an elementary school, that the teachers were sending home too many notes concerning their children's behavior and were requesting too many parent-teacher conferences. After checking a number of student records at random, you are inclined to agree with the parents.

At the next faculty meeting, you made reference to the PTA episode and your own observations. Little response came from the teachers, until one of the older teachers stated, "You recommended that we write anecdotal records on children so we do. If you had to handle some of these youngsters every day, you'd send home notes too. If the parents would do their job, it would make our job easier. I feel it is our responsibility to let the parents know in detail exactly how their children are getting along. It causes less headaches when report cards are sent home." Other teachers gradually join in with similar statements adding that the parents were responsible for the children's misbehavior and learning problems. A few teachers disagree, but are soon drowned out by the group who represent the majority of the faculty.

Assuming that some of these criticisms are valid, what might be done in planning a parent-teacher public relations program?

CASE 15

During the past year, you, the high school counselor, have not been able to function as effectively as you wished due to lack of qualified personnel. When this was brought to the attention of the Board of Education, they recognized the need, and created a new counseling position for the coming year. The principal has enlisted your aid in interviewing prospective candidates. Three people apply for the position, two of whom present excellent credentials in terms of education and experience.

The future looks bright until you are informed that the Board of Education has—for "personal reasons"—appointed the untrained candidate. How would you proceed in attempting to get either a clarification or reconsideration by the board? What does this appointment imply about the attitude towards guidance services in the school? What can be done in terms of public relations to demonstrate the need for professionally qualified personnel?

CASE 16

You are the director of pupil personnel services in a suburban school system that is in the process of rapid expansion because of the great influx of new residents into the town. Reorganization of many school programs becomes necessary in order to provide maximum service to the students.

At a recent meeting with the superintendent of schools, you and your staff were told that the superintendent had been thinking seriously about the most effective utilization of personnel. He feels that several counselors should be assigned to each class starting with the seventh grade. These counselors would move with the students from junior high school to high school, remaining with the class until it graduates. Your counselors receive this suggestion with lukewarm enthusiasm, and bring out a number of doubts about the desirability of such a plan both from the students' and their own viewpoints. You include your reservations with their reactions in a report to the superintendent.

Three days later, all guidance personnel in the system receive a memorandum from the superintendent stating that "I have decided upon further investigation that my proposal is sound. Anyone who feels himself unable to operate in this type of program will receive an excellent recommendation to seek a position elsewhere." What are the strengths and weaknesses of such a proposal? What are the problems inherent in the dictation of guidance policy by administration, especially when such policies may be in opposition to opinions of guidance personnel?

CASE 17

You are the director of guidance in a large suburban high school. At a parents' meeting the previous evening, a parent criticized the high operating costs of the local school system, emphasizing that the cost of the schools was amounting to 50 per cent of the community's annual budget. Another parent specifically referred to the cost of guidance services in the high school. He asked if this cost was justified in terms of an effective program.

You managed an answer last night, but you are now wondering just how effective your program really is. Since you would like to request additional funds for program expansion next year, it would help if you could know the present status of the program and could show critics some evidence of success. As a result, you have decided to evaluate your own and your staff's effectiveness and program. What criteria would you use? Who should be involved in such an evaluation and why?

CASE 18

Your state has recently passed a law requiring that parents be given access to their child's permanent record if they so request. As the director of guidance for a school system, you know that your records contain, among other things, test results, anecdotal records, and behavior summaries written by counselors.

You aren't too happy about the ruling, but you realize that you have no alternative but to abide by the law. You know that teachers will complain about having to defend their anecdotal records to parents, counselors will complain about violations of confidentiality, and parents will complain that they never knew much of the information in the record and they still can't understand most of it. How would you prepare for the inevitable deluge of requests and complaints from the members of your staff, the faculty, and the community?

CASE 19

You are the counselor for a junior high school containing about 900 students. The Board of Education of a neighboring community has been offering remedial and enrichment programs in their schools during the summer. Opportunities for attendance have been opened to surrounding communities, and recent statistics show that a large percentage of your students have enrolled each summer.

In the past, it was the policy of the summer school to provide each student and his school system with a complete evaluation of his performance at the end of the summer. This year, there was a change in administration, and it was decided to provide the students with a complete analysis of abilities including an IQ and other specific test scores. It has been the policy of your system not to release actual test scores, but rather to provide interpretations to parents and students.

Several parents have been positively impressed by the new policy of the neighboring system. They feel that for the first time they have been given a clear and accurate picture of their youngster's ability. They feel that your system should adopt the same practice.

Your principal recommends that you confer with the administrator of the summer program, and try to work out a plan that would be acceptable to all. What are the advantages and disadvantages of the policy being followed by the neighboring community? How would you proceed to advance the gains that are afforded many youngsters by this program, without penalizing those students who are unable to participate during the summer?

CASE 20

You are the director of guidance in a high school situated in the northern part of the country. This past winter has been one of the worst in history in terms of storms, icy roads, and hazardous conditions. As a result, a total of fifteen school days had to be cancelled. The Board of Education has asked the principal to submit a revised calendar to make up the missing days in order to meet state minimum attendance requirements. In reviewing the dates available in April, May, and June, it appears that the only solution is to conduct classes on Saturdays, and to eliminate spring vacation. The Board of Education accepts and approves this plan.

A number of complaints have come to you from parents, students, and teachers concerning possible conflicts. The principal has given you permission to excuse those students who present valid reasons. However, he first wants you to submit to him an outline of the criteria you will use so that he can issue a statement of procedure in the school paper. How would you go about setting up valid criteria that would be fair and objective to all students concerned, and still not destroy the effectiveness of the new ruling? Examine the conflicts inherent in the counselor's involvement in making or enforcing administrative decisions.

STUDENT LIFE AND ACTIVITIES

Cases 21–25 were selected to illustrate several of the problems relating to student life and student activities. Case 21 points up the issue of freedom with responsibility, and examines the role of the faculty advisor. Cases 22 and 23 revolve around the recurring problem of the role conflict for the personnel worker who is also asked to act as a disciplinarian. Cases 24 and 25 lead into an analysis of the responsibilities and options for self-government on the part of students.

CASE 21

You are the faculty advisor for a college newspaper. Throughout the year, you have tried to allow the staff complete freedom in running the paper. You have repeatedly emphasized that you have unlimited confidence in their sense of responsibility, and that you will not attempt to censor the paper in any way. The majority of the staff are journalism majors.

Recently, a member of the faculty was arrested on a morals charge. Upon his conviction, he was asked to resign from the faculty. At approximately the same time, an undergraduate girl gave birth to an illegitimate baby which she attempted to abandon in the rectory of a nearby church. Both stories received little mention in the public press. In glancing at the proofs for the forthcoming issue of the college paper, you see that the editors have included a complete report of both incidents, including the identity of the individuals concerned.

In checking with the editor, you are told that he feels that both stories represent news, and should be printed since they are matters of public record. You know that the paper is seen by many parents, and is sent to other colleges throughout the country as part of an exchange service. Considering the college and the individuals concerned, you do not think that either article should be printed. What is your responsibility to the college and to the students? What is the role of the faculty advisor in working with student activities?

CASE 22

You are director of guidance and advisor to the student council at a metropolitan high school. The student council has decided to sponsor a pre-Thanksgiving football dance in cooperation with their rivals from a nearby community. The dance would replace the previous rallies, canceled because of damage, trouble, and near-accidents in the past. All necessary details and clearances have been taken care of, and it appears that the dance should be a success in the opinion of all concerned.

Until eleven o'clock on the evening of the dance, the two groups from rival schools get along well, and there are no incidents. However, when the cheer leaders from the two schools attempt to lead the group in some team cheers, the gym becomes bedlam. Fireworks are set off in the gym and lights suddenly go out. The student council president, with the aid of the orchestra and the combined cheerleading squads, attempts to calm the group, but to no avail. The principal asks you to assist in restoring order, and to report to him any students who fail to comply with your requests. Examine the problems inherent in the duality of the counselor who is also a disciplinarian.

CASE 23

You are a college counselor who has recently been asked by a student group to serve as advisor to their fraternity. The college is primarily a campus college, with few commuting students. Recently, the administration put into effect stringent regulations prohibiting drinking, the entertaining of women above the first floor of any fraternity house, and the presence of women in a fraternity house after a twelve o'clock curfew.

A student came to you shortly after the rushing period ended and complained about drinking and women in the fraternity you are advising. He is bitter about not receiving an invitation to join, and you discount his story after the social chairman of the fraternity assures you it is false.

The following weekend is Homecoming, and as advisor and an alumnus of the fraternity, you are asked to serve as official chaperone at the dance. You spend a pleasant evening and see nothing out of order. At the end of the evening, the social chairman assures you that all women have left, and you depart shortly after twelve. Just before you arrive home, you remember that you left something at the fraternity house. When you arrive back at the house, you find the lights still blazing. Hearing some noise around the back, you investigate and find a rousing coed drinking party in progress. Going in the front door, you are met by a shapely coed who obviously doesn't recognize you. As you consider what action to take, keep in mind that if you report the fraternity to the administration, it will mean automatic suspension of the fraternity from campus and disciplinary probation for the entire group. Should the college counselor, if the choice is his, refuse to accept any role other than his own primary one?

CASE 24

You are the dean of students in a large campus college. Last night, while you were away, a group of some 200 men staged a wild "panty raid" on one of the girls' dormitories. Since your return, you have been receiving reports on what took place.

Evaluating the consequences, you find that the raid had had the following results: One man suffered a concussion when he fell from a window; several girls had to be treated for hysterics; the men caused about $700 damage to the dormitory and its furnishings; claims for missing personal belongings including several watches and rings have totaled another $300; the resident counselor in the girls' dormitory is threatening to resign; the town fire department is annoyed at the two false alarms turned in at the height of the raid; the town police are asking pointed questions about the lack of college discipline and the inefficiency of the campus police; and the local newspaper had spread the story over the front page with a picture of the raid at its peak being sent out over the wire services.

You have also discovered that the raid was instigated by a group from one particular dormitory, and was led by two men who have long been known leaders of this group. The two leaders are veterans who are due for graduation this spring and have respectable academic records up to this point. The president and several members of the board of trustees have already called on you to determine what action is to be taken. You have been given free rein. How can your handling of the situation provide a learning experience for all concerned? How might you prevent similar occurrences?

CASE 25

You are the guidance counselor in a private boys' school. It has long been school tradition to have a spring dance about a week before final examinations. In the past, girls have been invited as a group from a private girls' school nearby. The dance is held in the school gymnasium, and is eagerly anticipated by all students. The girls arrive in chartered buses, which for lack of a regular road to the gym, are forced to park in a lot about a quarter of a mile from the gym. There is a winding lane that meanders through an apple orchard from the parking lot to the gym, and it has been the custom for the boys to meet and serenade the girls when they arrive and to escort them to and from the gym.

For the past several years, there has been increasing criticism of the dances. These criticisms stress three points: First, that the lights in the gym are too low for proper chaperonage and couples disappear into dimly lit areas; second, that drinking has been prevalent; third, that during the traditional walk back to the buses after the dance couples get lost in the orchard and don't arrive for almost an hour.

The situation has reached the point where the headmaster has turned the problem over to you with the warning that unless similar occurrences are prevented this year, there will be no dances in the future. How would you handle the situation in the best interests of all concerned?

STUDENT HOUSING AND FOOD SERVICE

Cases 26–30 are concerned with the multi-faceted problems of housing and food service in residential settings. All deal with life on college and university campuses. Case 26 illustrates the problem of discipline within a residence hall. Case 27 points up the need for increased counseling proficiency on the part of a resident hall staff. Cases 28–30 deal with the administration of housing and food services, and the problems inherent in working with groups rather than with individuals.

CASE 26

You are the director of residences for a men's dormitory in a college located in an urban community. For the past several weeks, a series of firecracker explosions have been rousing residents in the middle of the night. Firecrackers of varying sizes have been set off in stair wells, outside staff doors, and in corridors at times between midnight and three A.M. The latest addition to the series has been the shooting of skyrockets up the stair wells.

Apart from the obvious problems of the disturbance to sleep, study, and the general atmosphere within the dormitory, you have become increasingly apprehensive about the danger to residents. Not only are some students emotionally unable to cope with such pranks for too long a period, but there are some physically handicapped and blind student residents who may be harmed. Your immediate feeling is that this has to stop. What successive steps would you take?

CASE 27

You are the counselor in an urban university which requires its students to reside either in one of the dormitories or in approved housing. During the first quarter, the director of a local girls' community residence calls you to report the negative behavior of one of your students. The student has violated curfew, been intoxicated, and placed unreasonable demands on personnel. You state your willingness to talk with the girl if the director makes the initial referral.

In a subsequent appointment made by the student, she relates how horrible the living conditions are, how mean the personnel have been, and how negative their attitudes are towards the university. Three days later, the student returns to tell you that she has been asked to leave the residence, and that she is being required to pay the room bill for the entire year. Keeping in mind your relationships with the director and the student, how would you proceed?

CASE 28

You are the dean of students in a small men's college. In previous years, undergraduates beyond the freshman year have been permitted to live in the nearby town if they wished instead of in dormitories or university-approved housing. In the interests of filling the dormitories, the board of trustees has just passed a ruling, effective the coming fall term, requiring all undergraduates to live in dormitories, fraternities, or approved housing.

As a result, the entire student body is up in arms, and decides to stage a protest demonstration with everyone sleeping on the campus lawn. This is carried out for one night. The next morning the story is published in all the metropolitan newspapers, and the college is faring none too well in the reports. From a personnel point of view, what suggestions would you make to prevent such reactions in the future? If called upon, what would you do to clarify the issues at hand?

CASE 29

You are an assistant to the dean of women at an urban university and have received an urgent call to report to one of the residence halls. When you arrive, a student meets you at the door and tells you that Mrs. Nyers, the head resident, is in her room with the college physician. Briefly, the student relates, "Apparently, some time during the dinner hour, someone broke into Mrs. Nyers' apartment and placed some white mice in her closet. When she returned from dinner, she noticed the lock broken and started to search her apartment to see if anything was missing. When she opened the closet and the mice ran out, she promptly became so hysterical that one of the students called you and the college physician."

The girls are milling around in the corridors, and everyone appears to be tense and waiting for the physician to come from Mrs. Nyers' apartment. As you are about to knock on the door, the college physician emerges. You talk briefly with Mrs. Nyers, and then leave in order to allow her to get some rest. The physician ask to speak to you confidentially. He informs you that he feels it was a shock, but that Mrs. Nyers should be all right by morning. However, he does feel that this could have been serious and recommends some action.

Since so many people seem to be involved, you decide to report the incident to the dean of women. She authorizes you to take immediate action to find out who was responsible. Not only is the incident itself disrespectful, but breaking and entering did take place. Some of the residents were not present at the time, while others have signed out since the incident. You have decided to have a house meeting with all residents at ten-thirty that evening to discuss the situation. What are some of the possible ways to approach this subject?

CASE 30

You are the dean of a small campus college. You have just been reading for the fifth time an editorial in the semi-weekly college paper sharply criticizing the food service in the college cafeteria. What makes the editorial so interesting is the knowledge that the entire student body has been boycotting the college cafeteria for two days because of the food being served. They have flatly refused to eat in the dining halls, and have been crowding into nearby off-campus diners for meals. Reports of the boycott have filtered out, and you have been receiving a flood of calls from irate parents, disturbed members of the governing board, and interested reporters. How would you interpret the individual's freedom of expression in light of an institution's right to establish regulations and set standards?

PART III

CRITICAL ISSUES: THE INDIVIDUAL

Often times have I heard you speak of one who commits
a wrong as though he were not one of you, but a
stranger unto you and an intruder upon your world.
But I say that even as the holy and righteous cannot
rise beyond the highest which is in each one of you,
So the wicked and the weak cannot fall lower than the
lowest which is in you also.

Kahlil Gibran,
The Prophet

The previous two sections have been concerned with the community and the school. Each has included cases which illustrate the pressures confronting the student personnel worker when these school and community relationships are examined. This third section is devoted to some current problems and issues which bear upon the individual as he pursues his daily life. Decisions based upon the question: Is it for the good of society or for the good of the individual? frequently end up caught in the quicksand of ambiguity. It is difficult to obtain agreement as to the definition of "good," since this depends upon the attitudes of the individual and the society in which he finds himself.

However, with clarification, we commonly find problem-solving and decision-making revolving around the question of whether or not a person will or should behave according to some expected pattern. The individual may be seen by others as himself, but, more frequently, he is regarded by others not as he *is* but as he should be according to the mores of society . . . either he conforms or he does not.

Counselors, administrators and teachers all speak of the worth of man, of the recognition of individual differences and democratic principles, and of the task of education in preparing youth for life in a democratic society. Yet, if the very system which "educates" youth is autocratic, fear-producing, and pressure-creating —if it forces youngsters to behave in ways which brand them in the eyes of society as deviates—then one can question if a free society of responsible people is ever to be realized. A society is a unit of individuals who have found some common considerations and agreed on some common purposes. During society's birth and growth, individuals are quickly divided into conformists and non-conformists. It is debatable whether or not all people can be categorized within only two groups. Are there not gray areas, or must everything be black or white? Cannot an individual disagree with a commonly accepted idea if he feels that acceptance would force him to compromise his beliefs? Is it possible that those who are willing to accept the label of "deviate" do so because they are secure within themselves and do not need the security of society?

The increased hostility and aggression towards teachers, the school, parents, and others are symptoms of youth's discontent and confusion, and should cause educators, especially the personnel worker, to reevaluate their practicing philosophies. If the role of the personnel worker is to be recognized and accepted as "professional," he cannot allow himself to function in a system where the very principles of human dignity are thwarted—where principles of learning are constantly contradicted or where the consideration of values is a coercive role. Although the authors, as counselor educators, are aware of the gaps between theory and practice, they do not feel their task is or should be to foster what is. The cases in this section have been developed for the specific purpose of initiating discussion in light of what one does in exercising the privileges of his particular job title, and what he feels he must do in order to maintain his status.

The work of the counselor is primarily developmental. He is expected to have a broad understanding of the needs of people as well as the needs of the environment, a definite set of competencies, and a depth and diversity of skills. The counselor's role in the prevention of mental illness and the advancement of mental health is emphasized when one realizes the important role of emotional responses—in teaching and learning and in educational and vocational planning—in fact in all aspects of daily life.

Fromm has stated,

> Our society is run by a managerial bureaucracy, by professional politicians; people are motivated by mass suggestions, their aim is producing more and consuming more, as purposes in themselves. All activities are subordinated to economic goals, means have become ends; man is an automaton—well fed, well clad, but without any ultimate concern for what is his peculiarly human quality and function.[1]

To what extent are personnel workers a type of "managerial bureaucracy" who speak about freedom but act in ways that deny its

[1] Erich Fromm, *The Art of Loving* (New York: Harper & Row, 1956), pp. 132–133.

existence? Guidance personnel frequently classify individuals through some test score or subjective evaluation. The school talks about democratic ways of living while contradicting these by the very nature of its autocratic structure. Is there such a person as an "overachiever" or a "stubborn child"? The authors think not, although an examination of many reports would indicate that some personne! workers feel justified in using these descriptions. The value of labels is limited, mainly because the individual who makes these judgments has failed to identify these as being so in *his* opinion only. Usually, the opinion of the "expert" is taken per se and some remedial action is determined accordingly. The personnel worker should be competent in understanding and administering a testing program that will help students plan academic programs and prepare for post-secondary experiences. Also, the counselor should recognize the limitations of descriptions associated with particular types of behavior—limitations which exist because of variations in social influences, beliefs and attitudes.

What is considered a deviation from some norm in one culture may be the expected behavior in another. The excellent writings of Margaret Mead, Ruth Benedict, and other anthropologists have encouraged the study not only of other cultures but also of our own for an understanding of man's values and judgments.

Too frequently, a diagnosis of man is based on the ways his actions can be interpreted, and little recognition is given to the importance of the evaluator's frame of reference. For instance, a person may be classified as a "transvestite" (one who wears the clothing of the opposite sex and for whom contact with such clothing offers gratification). Whether the person *is* such or *does* perform in this manner for such reasons, is often considered insignificant. His behavior is different, or at least a departure from the norm in our society, and thus the label is considered to be justified.

This example may seem somewhat extreme, but if one were to list the labels used to identify persons who show behavior different from the so-called normal, current vocabulary words would include: delinquent, underachiever, stubborn child, homosexual, cheat, liar, trouble-maker—to name but a few.

However, when such behavior is examined closely, it is found to resemble descriptions found under the general heading of "mental illness." That is, the maladjustment displayed by an individual is serious enough to deprive him of full acceptance in his particular society *even though his behavior may be a normal reaction to an abnormal situation.* The individual is considered not only harmful to himself but also to others, and is penalized for his deviation by ostracism by society.

Once one has said: Here is a person who needs some help, the question is: How well are student personnel workers equipped to understand the problem and to offer help? Intellectual knowledge of mental and emotional disturbance is insufficient; it must be accompanied by some self-understanding by the personnel worker if the labeled individual is to be helped to find acceptable and satisfying ways to cope with his anxieties.

If, as has been implied, testing or identifying people is not the personnel worker's concern the reader may be asking what *should* be his function? Let the authors emphasize that they cannot dictate to the reader, but, from their experiences with students in counselor preparation, they have found that the most apparent pressure is that of performing a task which does something *to* a person rather than helping him take some steps toward helping himself. For example, there has recently been much national emphasis on the problem of the school dropout. It is the opinion of the writers that such action is not a loss to society but to the individual who could find no other satisfactory way of coping with the immediate situation. Each June, statistics are presented locally and nationally of the number of persons who have been accepted for further educational programs. Rarely are follow-up studies reported to show the achievement of these plans. Getting people into colleges seems to be a major responsibility of school counselors; stimulating the intellect of the academically talented, another. Perhaps this function, bound by the past and preparing for the future with little appreciation for the present, is an area for consideration. What a person has been and what he can be receives much more focus than what he is at this particular moment. If one accepts Emerson's point that "Society everywhere is in conspiracy against the manhood of everyone of its members,"[2] then to foster this practice would appear to be bordering on unethical practice, especially in view of the verbalized "respect for man." Probably in no other relationship does the pressure of responsibility for decision-making have more meaning than in the one-to-one relationship.

The professional worker who has prepared himself for the counseling phase of the guidance program should have sufficient background in the various theories to create for himself a philosophy of counseling congruent with his own personality. Whatever self-concepts the counselor has identified for himself will be reflected and have an important part in his relationships with others.

Counseling is a unique, rare, and special experience in which one person shares with another his perceptions of the world and his place in it. The counselor has the major responsibility for communicating acceptance and understanding of both the counselee and his expressed or implied problems. Too little appreciation is given to the struggles of some counselees as they bare their deepest personal feelings. The focus of the relationship is frequently directed to the factors which appear to be the cause of the anxiety—parents, sex, religion, school, etc.—rather than towards the person who is seeking to return to a state of equilibrium. It seems strange to hear counselors discourse on the right and dignity of the individual and yet observe them denying an individual the freedom to analyze, explore, and express his own thoughts.

It is not unusual for the personnel worker to encounter situations in which maintaining a state of confidentiality is of prime importance. The ethics inherent in any counseling relationship represent an important concern to both the counselee and the counselor. The rationale, particularly for the school counselor, for violating the principle of confidentiality appears to relate more to the position of the counselor than to the welfare of the counselee. Efforts have been made by various professional organizations to define the ethical

---

[2] Ralph Waldo Emerson, *Self-Reliance* (Mount Vernon, N.Y.: Peter Pauper Press), p. 13.

role for the professional worker. As previously mentioned, the limitation to confidentiality lies in those instances where the counselee's frame of reference and behavior may be harmful to himself or to others. Not, as has been the case, where the counselor feels he may be risking his position when he has shared a counselee's deepest feelings of concern.

Conant's works *The American High School Today* and *Slums and Suburbs*[3] both propose guidelines for working with people who show certain test scores or exhibit categorized types of behavior. The statement "Education is for all" seems to have taken a different perspective today. Even the identification of the talented or creative is now the province of some "experts" who determine some set of standard behaviors by which a person avoids rejection. Perhaps we are not allowing individuals the freedom to be. Industry has the so-called alienated worker. To what extent do schools have the alienated student? Freedom to draw, write, or express oneself is easily discussed; yet in the final analysis, one is free to act only to the extent that the giver of such freedom is free to accept. This is particularly true in the practice of confidentiality.

Existing codes of ethics imply that one maintains privileged communication only so long as there is no danger to the counselor or to others. Who determines this limitation? The personnel worker? The individual? (We speak of the individual as a separate person; even Webster defines him as such, but, as these questions arise, still others emerge.) Would it not be more professional for the counselor to say: I am uncomfortable knowing this information and need to relate it to others, rather than rely on his personal evaluation of what society will or will not accept? It is interesting to note that society is usually brought into the frame of reference when the actions or details threaten the recipient of such information. In a profession which speaks so glibly of the positive side of man and his need for freedom to grow, it seems strange to see an increasing involvement in systems which tend to deny this aspect.

[3] James B. Conant, *The American High School Today* (New York: McGraw-Hill, 1959); *Slums and Suburbs* (New York: McGraw-Hill, 1961).

Knowledge of individual behavior is vital to a helpful relationship, if it comes from the individual concerned. The more he is able to share his perception of himself and his world, the more the personnel worker will be able to help him find the place he is seeking, and thus become a contributing person in his environment.

Frequently, the personnel worker interprets his responsibility as a mandate to change. One approach, used in single and group sessions, is to communicate the existing philosophy which both directly and indirectly points out the ways acceptance can be assured. Often, the results of these meetings do bring about change, but a closer look would show that the "changed" individuals were forced to find new ways to maintain their own sense of worth. Shouldn't a person be privileged to determine some limits for himself? In essence the student personnel worker is committed to people rather than to subjects who can be measured on a graph or even compared from one day to the next with themselves.

It is rather perplexing to witness the apparent readiness of personnel people and other adult models to manipulate and attempt to alter other human beings. What allows one to know what is best for another person? There are many people who feel comfortable giving advice, manipulating people, enforcing rules, etc. Must the personnel worker be one of these, or can his contribution in the relationship with another be unique? Can he provide a climate for change as the need and direction for change is initiated and determined by the individual? There is no one road toward a specific goal. However, when there is no choice of which road to travel, the journey will probably be unpleasant. Denying individuals the opportunity to make their own adaptations offers little hope that many people will realize self-reliance or self-respect. Counselor preparation based upon the concepts of the psychoanalytical, eclectic, developmental, learning theory, existential, or client-centered approach may serve as some basis for a helpful relationship, but, in the final analysis, the kind of person the counselor *is* may actually be the most important variable in the creation of an experience which will be a meaningful one for counselee and counselor alike.

COUNSELING: REFERRAL

The cases in this section were chosen specifically to illustrate many of the core problems confronting the personnel worker in a complex society. Cases 31–36 are concerned with methods and difficulties in the referral process. Case 31 describes a situation in which the concept of referral must first be explained to a parent. Cases 32 and 33 lead into ways and means of earlier referral of youngsters in difficulty. Case 34 points up the problems of referral and communication between the school and community agencies. Cases 35 and 36 deal with the multiple problems of counseling, maintaining confidentiality, and providing help when no need has been expressed directly by the individual who seems to need help.

CASE 31

You have recently been appointed coordinator of personnel services for the town's elementary schools. At one of your staff meetings, both the remedial reading teacher and the speech therapist ask to discuss the case of Robert Jennings.

As they share their knowledge of Robert, and evaluate him in terms of their professional experiences with him, it readily becomes apparent that there are many emotional problems involved. It seems that he needs treatment beyond that which can be provided by the school. Therefore, the three of you agree that Robert should be referred to a child guidance clinic for further study and help. The only complicating factor comes from the knowledge, gained from his cumulative record folder, that Robert's father is a practicing psychiatrist.

You notify the principal of the decision, but he refuses to be a part of it because of Robert's family background. He leaves the entire matter in your hands saying, "If you want to tell the shoemaker that his child is without shoes, go ahead."

The major issue here is Robert, but the ideal solution is to have Dr. Jennings realize Robert's need, and reach this same conclusion for himself. What are some of the identifying data which you should accumulate to aid in your conference with Dr. Jennings?

CASE 32

An increase in the number of juvenile offenders brought before the courts in your town has caused great concern among community leaders. The local chief of police has asked the town newspaper to print a summary of laws pertaining to juveniles. In addition, he has sent a letter to the school administration asking for cooperation.

The superintendent of schools asks you, as director of pupil personnel services, to study the laws, and to work out a set of warning signals for teachers in hopes of detecting pre-delinquents or actual delinquents who could be referred for treatment or legal action before the situation gets out of hand. He feels that you have knowledge of home background, students' behavior, and possible violations of laws. Although you have some reservations, you study the laws, and find two legal definitions that are particularly pertinent. These are: (1) The wayward child—a child between the ages of seven and seventeen who habitually associates with vicious or immoral persons or who is growing up under circumstances exposing him to lead an immoral, vicious or criminal life; and (2) the stubborn child—any minor who stubbornly refuses to submit to the lawful and reasonable commands of another whose commands said minor is bound to obey.

How would you interpret these two laws to teachers and other school personnel? How would you proceed in setting up an over-all program to prevent and detect juvenile delinquency?

CASE 33

Frank, a fifteen-year-old boy with normal intelligence as tested by the school psychologist, is the only child of a successful lawyer. He is very frail in appearance, and because of this timid look and the fact that he resembles the epitome of weakness, his classmates have come to make Frank the butt of classroom jokes.

Frank tries to hide his weak appearance by dressing and talking like a tough guy. The only problem with this facade is that Frank stutters very badly and his actions are considered very funny by the rest of the students. One of his teachers has brought this to your attention, expressing the feeling that something should be done as his stuttering is becoming more pronounced. How could you encourage earlier referral of such cases by school personnel? Explore the various ways of initiating contact with an individual without revealing a source of information.

CASE 34

You are the director of a community child guidance clinic. Since you took the position three years ago, you have been receiving an increasing number of referrals from the public schools. The schools do not have the personnel to provide the type of help needed by children and their parents, and the economic level of the community is low, so the board of education has voted to subsidize part of the cost for the treatment of such cases.

At a recent staff meeting, one of your therapists brought up the fact that the principal of one of her clients had requested a complete report on the child including diagnosis and treatment. The principal felt that this information was necessary for teachers to handle the youngster properly, since he was a constant discipline problem. When the therapist balked at revealing confidential information, the principal announced that he intended to complain to the board of education and would do all in his power to halt all financial aid from the schools to the agency. Other staff personnel reveal that they have had similar requests and complaints from other school personnel in recent weeks.

You realize that if the school stops subsidizing the fees for children, then the agency would have to increase the cost to the parents and this would force many families to stop treatment. What possible suggestions might you propose to meet the needs of the schools and maintain the necessary confidential aspects of the agency?

CASE 35

You are the director of a women's residence hall in a small coeducational college. One of the students comes to your apartment and talks of her concern for her roommate. Finally she admits that she is extremely upset about the rumors which have been circulating among some of her fellow students—specifically, that Joanne, her roommate, is pregnant. In telling you, she realizes that, if the rumor is true, the girl will automatically be dismissed from the college, according to clearly established policy.

Although you do not ask her directly about her actual knowledge of the situation, several inferences would lead you to believe that this girl feels her conclusions represent a definite probability. The student pleads with you to do something to either stop or confirm the rumor. She feels that her associations with others are being affected by such a possibility. In addition, if the situation actually exists and the roommate hears of the rumors, she is certain to accuse her of telling others. Evaluate the possible courses of action you feel you might pursue.

CASE 36

You are fulfilling the function of vocational and educational counselor in a school, and as such, you rarely get involved with personal problems. A fourteen-year-old student comes to your office and asks if she might talk with you. You suggest that if her problem is personal, perhaps she should see her clergyman or family physician (since there is no one else in the school), but she insists that she wishes to talk to you.

During her discussion, she tells you that one of her classmates needs help, as she severely abuses herself physically when she fails a test or does poorly in class. The student doesn't understand what is happening, and states that the girl's parents apparently are unaware of this behavior. She pleads for help in stopping these actions. How would you proceed in such a situation? What are the limitations in handling personal-emotional problems within the actual school setting?

COUNSELING: ETHICAL STANDARDS

Cases 37 and 38 revolve around counseling ethics—the corner-stone of counseling practice. Case 37 deals with the personnel worker's responsibility to the individual when it may conflict with a responsibility to society. Case 38 examines problems of an ethical nature, and explores approaches to methods of handling violations of professional ethics.

CASE 37

You are an educational placement officer for a large urban college. You have just completed an interview with a superintendent from a nearby community. While looking over the credentials of prospective teaching candidates, the superintendent asks you if the gentleman sitting outside the office is Edward King. You indicate that you hadn't noticed, but that the name is that of one of the college's former graduates. Without your asking, the superintendent informs you that he and Mr. King's principal suspected him of being an exhibitionist. As a result, King was asked to resign with the understanding that their suspicions would not be on his record, but that he should not request any recommendations from the school system.

The superintendent leaves, and your secretary informs you that Mr. King would like to see you about openings in other school systems since he has just submitted his resignation. Keeping in mind your responsibilities both to the college and to other graduates, what would you as the educational placement officer do?

CASE 38

You are the director of admissions for a small coeducational college with an excellent national reputation. During an interview with a prospective candidate, you note some discrepancies between the grades reported by the candidate and her official transcript sent by the school. In several instances, the transcript reports grades higher than those sent by the candidate. The candidate is at a loss to explain the discrepancy except to state that her report is correct.

In checking with the high school, you are referred to the high school counselor. The counselor suggests that he come to the college to discuss the matter in person. In a confidential conference, he tells you that the candidate in question is the daughter of the chairman of the local Board of Education. It seems that her father had threatened the counselor with loss of his job if the girl is not accepted to your college. As a result, he had altered the transcript, not knowing that the girl would report her actual grades. He pleads for your understanding and confidence. Several ethical questions are suggested by this report. Identify one or more and explain the type of action you would take in response to each.

COUNSELING: CONFIDENTIALITY

Cases 39–45 concern the issue of confidentiality as it affects the personnel worker in his daily practice. Case 39 illustrates the conflict of the counselor who is also responsible for discipline and rule enforcement. Case 40 raises the question of the obligation of confidentiality. To whom is the counselor responsible, the individual who has given him certain confidential information or the individual who may be injured by the suppression of that information? Cases 41 and 42 involve the duality of the teacher-counselor role and its relationship to areas of confidentiality. Case 43 explores staff relationships and sources of information. Cases 44 and 45 lead into the question of the counselor's obligations to the individual, the school, and the community when the three are in conflict.

CASE 39

You are a counselor at a small college. There have been many rumors floating around the campus among the staff, students, and alumni about homosexual activities among students on campus. The entire matter is of great concern to everyone, and an attempt is being made to obtain some evidence in order to take appropriate action.

As you are walking across campus one night, you accidentally stumble across two girls engaged in such activity. They quickly leave when they see you. The next morning, before you have had a chance to do anything, they come to you to ask that you not report them, since they are sure it will mean automatic expulsion and disgrace for their families. They also tell you why they engage in such activity, and that they know of at least thirty other students who also are overt homosexuals. The two girls are so frightened and desperate that they say they will expose every one of the others if you report them.

You know that it is practically impossible to keep expulsion proceedings quiet with such a large group involved, and that the college can ill afford such unfavorable publicity. You also know that the policy has already been set that this type of offense shall lead to the automatic expulsion of the offenders. How would you proceed to work with the students? How would you reconcile your responsibility to the individuals concerned and your responsibility to the college?

CASE 40

As the school counselor, you are automatically an ex officio member of the school's honor awards committee. This year, there is a tie for the top award, a four-year scholarship to the state university. Both students eligible for the award have obtained the same grades, and received identical scores on the College Entrance Examination Boards. Both are outstanding students, leaders in school activities, and have the respect of their classmates. In addition, both students would have extreme difficulty in meeting the financial obligations of college expenses without the scholarship aid. The committee is in a quandary, and is looking to you for suggestions.

For the past year, you have seen one of the two students for counseling other than academic. During the last session, he told you that he had someone else take the college board examinations for him. He is thoroughly ashamed of his action, and doesn't know why he did it, but he told you that he doesn't have the courage to admit this to anyone else since it would hurt his parents, teachers, and friends too much. What are the implications of knowing such information and maintaining the position of confidante?

CASE 41

You are a third-grade teacher with graduate training in guidance and counseling. Although you have no special guidance assignments, you frequently are called upon by other teachers and the principal when problem cases arise. Also many students have expressed the feeling that you are easy to talk with, and though they are not in your class, they frequently come to you on an informal basis for help.

At the end of a day, the daughter of one of your fellow teachers comes to you and, without any warning, starts to cry. She asks to tell you a secret and makes you promise not to let anyone know. You give her your promise, and then you learn her secret is: "I'm going to run away today. Mommy and Daddy are always fighting and I want to live with you."

You listen and encourage her to discuss her problem further. As you are talking together, her mother happens to walk by your room and sees Anne. She enters the room and, noticing Anne's tears, demands an explanation. Anne bursts out, "Remember, you promised."

What action would you take in order not to break your confidence with Anne, as well as not to hinder further the mother-daughter relationship? Would you try to work with Anne or would you refer her to someone else?

CASE 42

You are a faculty member in a program designed for the preparation of guidance personnel. Recently, several of your advisees have asked about the possibility of personal counseling for themselves. You suggest several possibilities including outside agencies, college counseling services, and other faculty members. One of your students states that since you are his advisor and he has gotten to know you in class, he would feel most comfortable being scheduled with you for counseling.

This problem is typical of the conflicts that can arise when one tries to fill the dual role of faculty-advisor and faculty-counselor, or when the counselee is the child of a close friend or colleague. What are the limitations, if any, to this type of counseling relationship? What decision would you reach, and how would you explain your decision to your advisee?

CASE 43

A small group of students, including several of the most popular and outstanding members of the class, have come to you, a high school teacher, and asked for your help in getting rid of the guidance counselor. It seems that she has been telling many students that she wants to counsel them because they have "personality problems." The group that comes to you have all received this information, and until now have just avoided her.

Lately, the counselor has been sending them notes stating that they must make appointments with her. The students appear frightened by her insistence, especially since they know she will be writing all of their recommendations for colleges and jobs. They do not feel free to speak to the principal, but hope you will do so, since you are their class advisor.

What are the ways that information of this nature can be communicated to a colleague in a helping way? Would such action be indicated in this case?

CASE 44

You, as school social worker, have been doing extensive work in one of the rapidly deteriorating sections of a large city. The area is sharply divided into several racial and immigrant groups. Most of the residents live in a constant state of overcrowding and poverty. Friction between families and groups is continual and explosive.

While making a home visit, you overhear several boys talking in the hallway about plans for tonight's attack against another neighborhood gang. One of the boys notices you and warns you to say nothing. What would you do, keeping in mind your responsibility to society, and the fact that you can help these people only so long as they trust you?

CASE 45

You are the director of guidance in a large urban high school. The Board of Education recently requested a team of evaluators from a nearby university to survey the physical facilities within the school system to determine their adequacy. The report on the high school revealed it to be old, badly overcrowded, and completely unsuitable for modern educational needs in terms of library space, classroom needs, and science education. The survey committee recommended that the building be completely replaced as soon as possible. Past attempts to obtain taxpayers' approval for a bond issue to finance a new building have been unsuccessful. Although the evaluation results have not been publicly announced, the findings have managed to become a major topic of conversation within the school. The Board of Education has already indicated its support for a new building.

One of your counselors has informed you that during a counseling session he has learned that the student body is organizing a strike to dramatize the need for a new building. You notify the principal, who tells you to investigate further and to take whatever action is necessary to handle the situation. How can you reconcile your responsibility to the school, your responsibility to the counselor, and his responsibility to his counselee?

SUMMARY

The authors believe that learning is a continuous process. Whether you are a neophyte still formulating a point of view about student personnel work, or a recognized expert with a working definition of your role, we feel these cases can be of value.

This above all: to thine own self be true,
And it must follow, as the night the day,
Thou canst not then be false to any man.

William Shakespeare,
Hamlet, Act I, Scene 3

APPENDIX

Partial transcript of group discussion using the case study approach (see p. 6).

Group members:

Tom: Liberal Arts, History; group leader

Betty: Elementary Education

Mary: Liberal Arts, English

Carol: Elementary Education

Jean: Education, Social Studies

The case assigned to the group:

You are the director of residences at a state-supported university. As such, you are responsible for taking night calls on any problem that occurs within the women's dormitories. At 10:30 one evening, you receive a call from the head resident of one of the dorms. She tells you that she has just talked with a freshman who stated that she and two of her roommates had searched the luggage of her fourth roommate and had found a loaded pistol and a full clip of ammunition.

The head resident states that she questioned the girls about their reasons for searching the personal property of another student. The answer given was: "We were worried about her. Ever since Christmas vacation she has been so depressed, and all she talks about is running away. We just wanted to see if her suitcase was packed." Further, the girl concerned had previously mentioned suffering from a nervous breakdown. To complicate matters, her roommates think she may be pregnant. The girl has returned to her room, but is unaware that her roommates know about the pistol. The girls left the pistol where they found it.

TOM: I thought the case was very serious and needed immediate attention—because at the very least she could commit suicide—at the most she could commit murder. She's got a gun with a full clip in it.

BETTY: That's true, but you're going on the assumption that the gun is going to be used for suicidal purposes. How do you know that the gun wasn't just there for—for safety purposes?

TOM: You don't know.

BETTY: You don't know, yet the first thing you—the first thing you said was—

MARY: But you have to realize that the residence counselor must be directly in charge of the dormitory where the incident occurred, and must be familiar with the girl, and there must be some element of doubt on her part to make her call you as residence director.

CAROL: Who would need a gun in a residence hall?

TOM: Hardly any of us need a gun really.

BETTY: Well, I knew a girl—[cut off]

MARY: Even if the gun was there for no purpose, there shouldn't be a gun there at all.

BETTY: Well, I know a girl who I went to school with who was carrying a gun with her because her father was—you know—she lived, she came from way out. And her father gave her this gun—got a permit and everything just to keep for safety purposes—and the school was not involved because he knew the school would take it away from her or something, so—

TOM: Yes, but there's another factor—she's a pretty depressed person—supposedly.

BETTY: Well, another thing—the trouble with girls—you know how it is, well, well these three girls who discovered all this—they, they discovered the gun and immediately—ha, she's going to kill herself, and they thought of all these things—

TOM: I think they were wrong—excuse me.

BETTY: Oh this girl, she must be depressed and they, they were bored and just wanted to start something—

MARY: But why did they have to get in touch with the director of residences and by the time it got there why not ask someone who really knew the situation as the head resident of the dormitory?

CAROL: Well she hasn't helped in other situations.

MARY: She should be familiar with it.

CAROL: In our dorm there are 500 girls—now the head resident doesn't know many of the girls and if they were nervous or if they had a breakdown and it wasn't on their record—

MARY: Well, in our dormitory, they'd be told, they'd first get the resident assistant since she knows the girls she's in charge of.

TOM: I think it's worse—

CAROL: Oh—well that depends on the resident assistant—she wasn't aware of many situations on our floor. [group laughs] Well, Tom, what were you going to say?

TOM: No—go ahead—I'm just one of the group.

CAROL: No, I'm just saying that not—that this doesn't mean that anyone has to know what was going on.

BETTY: What made the girls go in the first place to look for the gun? There must have been something—

MARY: She had a nervous breakdown and was depressed—I'll go along with that.

TOM: I think the girl, the poor kid, has shared some confidence and when she gets back—this feeling of closeness wasn't there anymore and they noticed depression—but I think they were wrong not going to the head resident in the first place and telling her they noticed these things. You're against searching the bag, but the fact is they have found the gun and the girl is depressed.

CAROL: Yes—well, this is what they say—but as director of residences I would need more proof of this than just what was said.

TOM: I wouldn't.

MARY: I would.

TOM: I wouldn't.

MARY: I'd want it coming immediately because human life is the most important thing.

CAROL: True, yes, but first of all I want to talk with the girl myself and if I noticed anything wrong—

TOM: There's not time.

CAROL: And if I noticed anything wrong or out of the way—uh—

MARY: By the time you got to her she may have used the gun.

CAROL: Oh no—they already had found the gun and the gun was still sitting there.

MARY: But look—if she's thought of using the gun, she could certainly think of other ways.

BETTY: I said that I would have her, as soon as she gets back— tell her that the head resident wants to see her—right away.

TOM: I would get over there myself as fast as possible—and another thing—uh—

BETTY: Why give the girl a heart attack—she's already—

CAROL: Maybe it's just circumstantial evidence—have you seen people committed for murder because—

MARY: Committed doesn't mean anything.

CAROL: It does.

TOM: Yes but it does—it does because—

MARY: Maybe the girl is afraid of having a nervous breakdown.

JEAN: Shall I tell you what my nutty idea was?

TOM: Yes.

JEAN: I said the first thing I would do would be go over and make sure the gun was blank—therefore nothing could happen—therefore—

TOM: You could hurt yourself with blanks.

JEAN: How much—you might get a powder burn.

TOM: More than that—it could ruin a person's face. What if she shoots herself?

BETTY: What would you do—what would you do? Take the gun away immediately?

JEAN: I said I would thank the girls for the information—ask them not to mention the incident again—least of all to the girl involved, and I in turn would not reveal their unorthodox searching—which was unorthodox—after all they shouldn't have been up there in the first place.

TOM: I don't agree on that.

JEAN: Then I would say—at the next possible chance, maybe that night or if there wasn't time, the next day—of course I don't know what would happen during the night.

TOM: There might not be another chance. But you can't tell—it's all a chance.

MARY: Suppose she came in from a date with a boy or something and decided that this was the night she was going to commit suicide—now you'd have it on your conscience the next morning that you didn't do anything—you waited till the next morning and the girl was dead.

TOM: There's always the possibility that she might act as soon as she comes in. I think I'd get the girls out of the room and ask them not to discuss it with anyone and try and get there myself as director of residences and detain her—and after that I'd call her parents—You know the problem is—

JEAN: That I can't do.

BETTY: I wouldn't call her parents, I feel that if she wanted her parents to know she'd have told them over Christmas or else she could have told them right then and there.

TOM: Yeah, but the problem involves more than school though—it involves her parents, probably her boy friend if they suspect her pregnancy.

JEAN: Well I think the head resident first should discuss it with her, and then see if she wants them to notify her parents. That might be the one thing she doesn't want yet, and since she has solved it herself or thought of something.

TOM: Yes, but she needs help.

JEAN: But how do you know her parents are the kind that could help her?

TOM: Yeah—but are you actually responsible for this girl? What if you do something and her parents go completely against what are you doing?

BETTY: But I don't think we should go behind this girl's back. I think that's one of the points that we always—

TOM: No, I would tell—No, I would tell her that we found the gun, and that we had reports that she's depressed. I think I would face her with these things.

JEAN: What, what if her mother is a crazy person—what if, what if that's the one thing she didn't want to do is to, is to let her mother know?

TOM: That's what I'm saying. Other people are responsible for this—It's not the school's responsibility for this alone.

JEAN: I disagree—she's at school and the school has to handle it.

TOM: Yeah, but these things—it might have happened away from school—it might have happened at home.

JEAN: Well it didn't—that's the point of it—it's at school so it's the school's—the school has the first chance to handle it.

CAROL: I think we're working on circumstantial evidence. I, I still feel that we should get more evidence to the fact that there is something wrong.

TOM: How?

CAROL: I'd, I'd have a conference with her and if I, if I discovered something, you know she probably wouldn't come right out and say "Oh, I'm going to kill myself." If I discovered anything in this—you know if she happened to come out and say "Well, I've been doing very poor in my work— I'm very disappointed and all in this," I would go to the school psychologist or the counselor and have her talk with her and—

TOM: Would you take the gun away?

MARY: What if she wouldn't come to you?

BETTY: What would you do with the gun? First thing I'd do is—

MARY: I'd take it.

JEAN: I'd lock the luggage room.

TOM: Do we agree that we would take the gun?

CAROL: No, I—you know when I first wrote this I said to take the gun and then as I was writing it I said after I realize—

BETTY: And how would she react when she didn't find the gun?

CAROL: Well at first I'd have her speak to the head resident and see if she'd speak to me, say if I was head resident—if she didn't speak to me—if she wouldn't talk about it all and say "It's my business"—then I'd tell her that they found the gun, because I don't feel like to just let her go back and just have the gun in the suitcase.

BETTY: Well the question is—what if she went there that night and you didn't have a chance to call her over or anything—and she went there and didn't find the gun—that would throw her into a real—

MARY: No, she could commit suicide another way too—

TOM: I think everything should be out in the open with her.

CAROL: I wrote in my paper that you could take the gun away; then she might cut her wrist with a razor blade.

BETTY: Yes, that might really do it.

JEAN: Why not lock the luggage room?

TOM: I think she should be taken into detention, almost forcefully and then notify her parents.

MARY: Yeah, but if you do that—if there was nothing wrong to begin with—something could develop.

JEAN: But you're acting like she's insane.

TOM: No, I'm not—I'm really not—yeah, but if we tell her that we've taken the gun—that we're aware that she's uh, uh depressed, that we've had reports that she's depressed.

MARY: When you go and tell someone that, they begin to wonder about it themselves even if nothing's wrong to begin with.

TOM: So if we leave her alone, there's other methods of killing herself—just like they said—she could break a glass in the room and cut her wrists—she could jump out a window;

she could hang herself on a light cord—I think she would have to be detained.

MARY: You'd have to do something for her, because as director of the residence you're in charge of all the girls, not just this one individual.

JEAN: But how about getting her roommates to work with you? And keeping somebody with her all the time.

TOM: Yeah, I agree with that—until when though? Then what would you do?

CAROL: But then you're putting the responsibility on one of the roommates, and suppose she does commit suicide?

JEAN: No I'm not saying that—I'm saying until you get a chance to talk with the girl, make sure—

TOM: What are you going to do with the gun though?

JEAN: Well I said I'd fill it with blanks—I don't know whether this is—

TOM: She could hurt herself—she really could.

JEAN: All right then—then I'd lock the luggage room.

BETTY: The luggage room is not that personal—it would be just kind of—I mean if she did go it would be that the whole luggage room is locked; it's not somebody—

TOM: Yeah, but she might want to do this right now—I think she should be told that we found the gun. You know being a head resident you would probably be aware of some of these problems coming along and I'd think you'd have names and numbers of professional help. I'd think you'd have to call someone, but I still think you'd have to detain the girl. Have, you know, maybe have yourself stay there with another person—and then I'd call the parents.

CAROL: Yeah, but then you jeopardize her so-called friends or roommates—She'd probably feel that these girls were sneaking around her luggage and lose those friends.

BETTY: I want to bring up the point about the parents. How do you know that these parents are normal? You're assuming that these parents are your parents or somebody.

TOM: Who said my parents are normal?

BETTY: I'm just saying that these parents are rational people—
How do you know maybe the one person she doesn't want
to tell is her mother—I don't think that's fair—to just go
and talk to her parents without speaking to her first and
see what she said.

TOM: I would speak to her first, but I would still notify her
parents.

CAROL: Well I don't think—maybe it's right to ask her about the
gun—just calm. Calmly ask her when she comes in—because it isn't really a normal thing to have girls carrying
guns around with them—and the gun should be confis-
cated just from a safety point of view . . . for everybody.

BETTY: Well, how would you have found out about it? That's the
thing, to explain that.

CAROL: That's the problem but then you'd be jeopardizing those
girls who found it and she'd feel badly about the girls
sneaking around. How would you like someone sneaking
in your luggage?

(later, in subsequent session)

JEAN: Let's take solutions . . . we are all assuming the worst.

TOM: Yeah, I think we have to assume the worst.

JEAN: You have to assume the worst as the resident director, and
then you have to get rid of the gun in some way. You
can't leave a loaded gun—because it's not just your own
life that you're endangering and after all her own life
is worth something too.

TOM: Yeah, you know what I did on my paper on my approach?
I divided it up into three areas: First I just took the case
generally; then I had thoughts before any action was
taken; then I had action taken.

JEAN: What action did you take?

TOM: Well the first action was take the gun. Then I would take
her roommates out of the room and I would try and be
there myself with the head resident.

JEAN: I think you should meet her downstairs.

TOM: Really?

CAROL: Yes, watch for her when she comes in.

TOM: What if she made a scene though, what if there's all kinds of people around there?

JEAN: No, I think it can be very subtle—you can be sitting on the couch or something—you know the lounges they have around the doorway—and when she comes in and starts walking towards the place, you walk over to her and say "Could I talk with you for a few minutes?"

CAROL: Or just make small talk, or invite her out for coffee, or something.

TOM: What if you brought up some other small infraction that she may have committed?

JEAN: What if she hasn't? I think you should be honest with the girl.

TOM: Oh, I agree with that in the first place, but if you want to meet her in the lobby, how are you going to do it?

MARY: Walk up and say "I'd like to see you."

BETTY: Be casual: Say "Would you come over to my office or . . ."

TOM: What if she says "What do you want?"

BETTY: I'd just say "I'd like to talk with you."

CAROL: What if she says . . . what if she says "Oh I'm busy . . . I'll, I'll . . ."

BETTY: If you walked in and the resident head came up to you and said "May I speak with you" in kind of, you know, a definite way, you—

TOM: Yeah, but this girl isn't acting in a normal pattern now.

JEAN: No, but I think you have to . . . if she says "I would rather not talk now, I have a headache" I would say "I think it's quite important that we do talk now and I really would like you to." I mean, what girl can back down after pressure like this . . .

CAROL: You know you said she wasn't acting in a normal pattern . . . I know people who have had nervous breakdowns—

TOM: But carrying a gun?

CAROL: Well, aside from that, the nervous breakdown doesn't mean that a person isn't normal now.

TOM: Yeah, I agree but she is carrying a gun and I don't consider that a normal action.

BETTY: Well I think that we sort of asked enough. I don't think we are getting anywhere anymore.

TOM: Well, if we could make some—some conclusions then . . .

JEAN: All right, then take the gun or in some way try and get her to talk—anyway call her in and talk with her that night.

CAROL: And then what would you do?

TOM: Would you detain her that night?

MARY: Depending on her reactions, I would think . . .

TOM: Where would she sleep that night? Would she sleep in her room?

JEAN: I'd take, I'd take her to the infirmary or someplace.

TOM: All right—so she wouldn't go back to her room.

JEAN: So she would not go back to her room, except to let her get her pajamas, toothbrush and all this stuff.

TOM: Would you let her roommates discuss this with anyone else?

CAROL: But the poor girl—what if she hasn't—what if she has— the poor girl . . .

TOM: But we can't, we can't go along that—

CAROL: You can't, we have to—

MARY: It all depends upon what she is going to say to you.

TOM: But there's one person—here's one person capable of killing about five other people—

MARY: Wait a minute, though: The point is whether she's going to say to you, she's going to tell the whole story to you when you speak with her, or she's going to say nothing. If she tells you the whole story then there might not be any need, if you can, sort of, calm her down . . . it depends upon what happens in that conversation which we do not know. So that's where we start.

JEAN: All right, now let's assume that she does talk with you.

What would you do then? Would you let her go up to her room?

MARY: Well, what does she say?

JEAN: Well, all right, she tells the whole story: She says, "I'm pregnant . . . I don't want to talk . . . I don't want you to tell my parents right now . . . I'd rather talk with them some other time when I have a little more confidence in myself," and she said "Yes, I was thinking of committing suicide."

CAROL: Was she very calm, just the way you are?

JEAN: Well, she'd be crying and nervous, probably.

TOM: Most likely she would be.

MARY: If you could sort of help her after she breaks down and let her get it out of her system, well, then maybe she could go back to her room and you wouldn't have to drag her out of her room and make her feel like she's—like she's some kind of a . . .

TOM: Well, I didn't intend to drag her out of her room; I just intended not to have her roommates there when she gets back.

MARY: Well, now I think if it's all sort of talked out I think she could go back to her room; but if she said nothing to you, well, then—

JEAN: I think you should take her to the infirmary or someplace where she can be under surveillance.

BETTY: I do too. Well, you could do this for her own good—I mean this is what they usually do.

TOM: Yeah, it's all for her own good, but it's also for the good of the school, too.

BETTY: Yeah, but you primarily want to approach her, I think, for her own good, and if you say, "Look, you're disturbed, you're upset right now, and don't you think it would be good if you could just get away by yourself and get some rest and we could discuss this further without the interference of going to class and studying and being around the other girls?"

JEAN: I think that's it. Let's call it quits there.

TOM: And that's about as far as this person can go—right? . . . because he has not. . .

JEAN: I don't think you can finish the whole case yourself. . . We don't know what really went on, and I think this is about as far as we can take it.

BIBLIOGRAPHY

Guidance: An Overview

Arbuckle, Dugald S. *Pupil Personnel Services in American Schools.* Boston: Allyn and Bacon, 1962.

Crow, Lester D., and Alice Crow. *Readings in Guidance.* New York: David McKay, 1962.

Farwell, Gail F., and Herman J. Peters (eds.). *Guidance Readings for Counselors.* Chicago: Rand McNally, 1960.

Guidance: An Examination. Harvard Educational Review. Vol. XXXII, No. 4. (Fall 1962).

Hatch, Raymond. *Guidance Services in the Secondary Schools.* Dubuque, Iowa: W. C. Brown, 1963.

Humphreys, A. Anthony, Arthur E. Traxler, and Robert D. North. *Guidance Services.* Chicago: Science Research Associates, 1960.

Johnson, Walter F., Buford Stefflre, and Ray Edelfelt. *Pupil Personnel and Guidance Services.* New York: McGraw-Hill, 1961.

Lloyd-Jones, Esther. *Behavioral Science and Guidance: Proposals and Perspectives.* New York: Bureau of Publications, Columbia Teachers College, 1963.

McDaniel, H. B. *Guidance in the Modern School.* New York: Dryden Press, 1956.

McDaniel, H. B., John E. Lallas, James E. Saum, and James L. Gilmore. *Readings in Guidance.* New York: Henry Holt, 1959.

Miller, Frank W. *Guidance: Principles and Services.* Columbus, Ohio: Charles E. Merrill, 1961.

Moser, Leslie, and Ruth Moser. *Counseling and Guidance.* Englewood Cliffs, N.J.: Prentice-Hall, 1963.

National Society for the Study of Education, *Personnel Services in Education.* 58th Yearbook, Part II. Chicago: University of Chicago Press, 1959.

Peters, Herman J., and Gail F. Farwell. *Guidance: A Developmental Approach.* Chicago: Rand McNally, 1959.

Peters, Herman J., and Riccio, Anthony C. *Guidance in the Elementary School.* New York: Macmillan, 1963.

Roeber, Edward. *The School Counselor.* Washington: The Center for Applied Research, 1963.

Rosecrance, Francis C., and Velma D. Hayden. *School Guidance and Personnel Services.* Boston: Allyn and Bacon, 1960.

Wrenn, C. Gilbert. *The Counselor in a Changing World.* Washington: American Personnel and Guidance Association, 1962.

Zeran, Franklin R., and John E. Lallas. *Guidance: Theory and Practice.* New York: American Book Co., 1964.

ORGANIZATION AND ADMINISTRATION

Andrew, Dean C., and Roy D. Willey. *Administration and Organization of the Guidance Program.* New York: Harper and Bros., 1958.

Ferguson, Donald G. *Pupil Personnel Services.* Washington: The Center for Applied Research, 1963.

Hatch, Raymond N., and Buford Stefflre. *Administration of Guidance Services.* Englewood Cliffs, N.J.: Prentice-Hall, 1958.

Zeran, Franklin R., and Anthony C. Riccio. *Organization and Administration of Guidance Services.* Chicago: Rand McNally, 1962.

PERSONNEL SERVICES IN HIGHER EDUCATION

Arbuckle, Dugald S. *Student Personnel Services in Higher Education.* New York: McGraw-Hill, 1953.

Feder, Daniel, *et al. The Administration of Student Personnel Programs in American Colleges.* Washington: American Council on Education, 1958.

Mueller, Kate H. *Student Personnel Work in Higher Education.* Boston: Houghton Mifflin, 1953.

Rackham, Eric N. *Student Personnel Services Inventory.* Kent, Ohio: Kent State University, 1963.

Williamson, E. G. *Student Personnel Services in Colleges and Universities.* New York: McGraw-Hill, 1961.

COUNSELING: THEORY AND PRACTICE

Adams, James F. *Problems in Counseling: A Case Study Approach.* New York: Macmillan, 1962.

Arbuckle, Dugald S. *Counseling: An Introduction.* Boston: Allyn and Bacon, 1961.

Bordin, E. S. *Psychological Counseling.* New York: Appleton-Century-Crofts, 1955.

Boy, Angelo V., and Gerald J. Pine. *Client-Centered Counseling in the Secondary School.* Boston: Houghton Mifflin, 1963.

Burton, Arthur (ed.). *Case Studies in Counseling and Psychotherapy.* Englewood Cliffs, N.J.: Prentice-Hall, 1959.

Byrne, Richard. *The School Counselor.* Boston: Houghton Mifflin, 1963.

Cottle, William C., and N. M. Downie. *Procedures and Preparation for Counseling.* Englewood Cliffs, N.J.: Prentice-Hall, 1960.

Evraiff, William. *Helping Counselors Grow Professionally.* Englewood Cliffs, N.J.: Prentice-Hall, 1963.

Loughary, John W. *Counseling in Secondary Schools.* New York: Harper and Bros., 1961.

McGowan, John, and Lyle Schmidt. *Counseling: Readings in Theory and Practice.* New York: Holt, Rinehart & Winston, 1962.

Patterson, C. H. *Counseling and Psychotherapy.* New York: Harper and Bros., 1960.

Peters, Herman J., Bruce Shertzer, James B. Heck, Richard R. Stevee, and Ralph E. Van Atta. *Counseling: Selected Readings.* Columbus, Ohio: Charles E. Merrill, 1962.

Rogers, Carl R. *On Becoming a Person.* Boston: Houghton Mifflin, 1961.

Standal, Stanley W., and Raymond J. Corsini. *Critical Incidents in Psychotherapy.* Englewood Cliffs, N.J.: Prentice-Hall, 1959.

Steimal, Raymond. *Psychological Counseling of the Adolescent.*

Washington: Catholic University of America Press, 1963.

Tyler, Leona E. *The Work of the Counselor.* 2nd ed., New York: Appleton-Century-Crofts, 1961.

Warters, Jane. *Techniques of Counseling.* New York: McGraw-Hill, 1964.

Williamson, E. G. *Counseling Adolescents.* New York: McGraw-Hill, 1950.

STUDENT ACTIVITIES

Frederick, Robert W. *The Third Curriculum.* New York: Appleton-Century-Crofts, 1959.

Gruber, Frederick C., and Thomas B. Beatty. *Secondary School Activities.* New York: McGraw-Hill, 1954.

Kilzer, Louis R., Harold Stephenson, and H. Orville Nordberg. *Allied Activities in the Secondary School.* New York: Harper and Bros., 1956.

Lunn, Harry H. (ed.). *The Student's Role in College Policy Making.* Washington: American Council on Education, 1957.

McKown, Harry C. *Extracurricular Activities.* 3rd ed., New York: Macmillan, 1959.

Miller, Franklin A., James H. Moyer, and Robert B. Patrick. *Planning Student Activities.* Englewood Cliffs, N.J.: Prentice-Hall, 1956.

GROUP GUIDANCE

Bany, Mary. *Classroom Group Behavior.* New York: Macmillan, 1964.

Beal, George M., Joe M. Bohlen, and J. Neil Raudabaugh. *Leadership and Dynamic Group Action.* Ames, Iowa: Iowa State University Press, 1962.

Glanz, Edward C. *Groups in Guidance.* Boston: Allyn and Bacon, 1962.

Kemp, Gratton. *Perspectives in the Group Process.* Boston: Houghton Mifflin, 1964.

Patterson, C. H. *Counseling and Guidance in Schools.* New York: Harper and Bros., 1962.

Warters, Jane. *Group Guidance.* New York: McGraw-Hill, 1960.

MEASUREMENT AND EVALUATION

Ahmann, J. Stanley, and Marvin D. Glock. *Evaluating Pupil Growth*. Boston: Allyn and Bacon, 1958.

Anastasi, Anne. *Psychological Testing*. 2nd ed., New York: Macmillan, 1961.

Baron, Denis, and Harold Bernard. *Evaluation Techniques for Classroom Teachers*. New York: McGraw-Hill, 1958.

Berdie, Ralph F., Wilbur L. Layton, Edward O. Swanson, and Theda Hagenah. *Testing in Guidance and Counseling*. New York: McGraw-Hill, 1963.

Chauncey, Henry, and John E. Dobbin. *Testing: Its Place in Education Today*. New York: Harper & Row, 1963.

Committee on Measurement and Evaluation. *College Testing*. Washington: American Council on Education, 1959.

Cronbach, Lee J. *Essentials of Psychological Testing*. 2nd ed., New York: Harper and Bros., 1960.

Findley, Warren (ed.). *The Impact and Improvement of School Testing Programs*. Chicago: National Society for the Study of Education, 63rd Yearbook, 1963.

Freeman, Frank S. *Psychological Testing*. 3rd ed., New York: Holt, Rinehart & Winston, 1962.

Froelich, Clifford D., and Kenneth B. Hoyt. *Guidance Testing*. Chicago: Science Research Associates, 1959.

Gerberich, J. Raymond, Harry A. Greene, and Albert N. Jorgensen. *Measurement and Evaluation in the Modern School*. New York: David McKay, 1962.

Goldman, Leo. *Using Tests in Counseling*. New York: Appleton-Century-Crofts, 1961.

Lyman, Howard. *Test Scores and What They Mean*. Englewood Cliffs, N.J.: Prentice-Hall, 1963.

Nunnally, Jum C. *Test and Measurements: Assessment and Prediction*. New York: McGraw-Hill, 1959.

Stanley, Julian C. *Measurement in Today's Schools*. 4th ed., Englewood Cliffs, N.J.: Prentice-Hall, 1964.

Thorndike, Robert L., and Elizabeth Hagen. *Measurement and*

Evaluation in Psychology and Education. 2nd ed., New York: Wiley and Sons, 1961.

Traxler, Arthur. *Measurement and Research in Today's Schools*. Washington: American Council on Education, 1961.

Tyler, Leona. *Tests and Measurements*. Englewood Cliffs, N.J.: Prentice-Hall, 1963.

Vernon, Philip E. *Intelligence and Attainment Tests*. New York: Philosophical Library, 1961.

STUDENT HOUSING

Riker, Harold C. *Planning Functional College Housing*. New York: Bureau of Publications, Teachers College, Columbia University, 1956.

THE SCHOOL AND SOCIETY

Conant, James B. *The American High School Today*. New York: McGraw-Hill, 1959.

Dahlke, H. Otto. *Values in Culture and Classroom*. New York: Harper and Bros., 1958.

Erikson, Erik. *Childhood and Society*. 2nd ed., New York: W. W. Norton, 1963.

Gordon, Ira J. *The School as an Agency of the Culture*. New York: Harper and Bros., 1956.

Kelly, Janet A. *Guidance and Curriculum*. Englewood Cliffs, N.J.: Prentice-Hall, 1955.

Packard, Vance. *The Status Seekers*. New York: David McKay, 1959.

Packard, Vance. *The Naked Society*. New York: David McKay, 1963.

Stearns, Harry L. *Community Relations and the Public Schools*. Englewood Cliffs, N.J.: Prentice-Hall, 1955.

Warters, Jane. *Changed Schools*. New York: McGraw-Hill, 1956.

FILMS

Angry Boy. International Film Bureau, Chicago, Ill. 33 minutes.

Boundary Lines. McGraw-Hill, New York. 10 minutes.

Breakdown. National Film Board of Canada. 42 minutes.

Counselor in a Changing World. American Personnel and Guidance Association, Washington. 30 minutes.

Feelings of Depression. National Film Board of Canada. 32 minutes.

Feeling of Hostility. National Film Board of Canada. 33 minutes.

Feeling of Rejection. National Film Board of Canada. 21 minutes.

High Wall. McGraw-Hill, New York. 32 minutes.

Howard. National Film Board of Canada. 30 minutes.

Joe and Roxy. National Film Board of Canada. 30 minutes.

Lonely Night. International Film Bureau, Chicago, Ill. 62 minutes.

Out of Darkness. McGraw-Hill, New York. 55 minutes.

Over Dependency. National Film Board of Canada. 32 minutes.

A Day in the Night of Johnathan Mole. National Film Board of Canada. 33 minutes.

Picture in Your Mind. McGraw-Hill, New York. 16 minutes.

Quiet One. Athena Films, New York. 67 minutes.

Shyness. National Film Board of Canada. 23 minutes.

Step by Step. International Film Bureau, Chicago, Ill. 20 minutes.

Stigma. National Film Board of Canada. 20 minutes.

Stress. National Film Board of Canada. 11 minutes.

To Serve the Mind. National Film Board of Canada. 25 minutes.

Who Is Sylvia. National Film Board of Canada. 27 minutes.

PRINTED IN U.S.A.